MW00830706

THE ART OF
SELLING

We Make Order Makers, Not Order Takers

ALISON MULLINS

Copyright © 2023 All rights reserved.
ISBN:
ISBN-13:

This book is dedicated to Roger and Lois Mullins
for enduring and encouraging all my crazy.

GET YOUR FREE GIFT!

TO GET THE BEST EXPERIENCE WITH OUR BOOK,
DOWNLOAD THE FREE WORKBOOK.
IMPLEMENT TECHNIQUES FASTER,
PUT THIS KNOWLEDGE TO ACTION.

"THE ART OF SELLING"

FREE DOWNLOAD
USE THE CODE: FREEWORKBOOK

WWW.REPMETHODS.COM
JOIN US!

TABLE OF CONTENTS

Section 1: Brand Management

Section 2: Lead Management

Section 3: Sales Process—On Your Mark, Get Ready, Sell

Section 4: Post-Sale Foundations

PREFACE

Twenty-plus years of working in sales and marketing will get you three things: a big ego—pummeled daily by the difficulties of wins and losses—a tired body from the hours spent driving, flying, and spending time away from home, and above all, a worn-out mind, tired of the chase and searching for a chance to slow down and have my cake and eat it too. Successful salespeople look at the world through the lens of wins and losses. Everything becomes competition; after all, we are natural competitors. It's a trait that is fundamental to success in the field. Our motivation comes from pursuing excellence, achieving goals, and surpassing targets.

But if we aren't careful, salespeople can burn out quickly. We can start to misuse things to try and close the next big deal. We could misuse drugs, alcohol, nicotine, pills, or other substances which become our coping mechanism in the highs and the lows of selling. We could misuse people, places, and even so-called healthy practices! Misusing any of this isn't healthy. So, we must work and search for balance and healthy coping mechanisms to sustain our careers. We must build stability and structure in our daily lives. We must live for the drive, the chase, the feeling. Enter my own sabbatical of 2023. In 2020 I accepted a new way of living. And in 2023 I'm developing a new way to love myself, to sell what I've got to give, to continue to learn, and to love more of what I do every single day.

About me

I'm Alison Mullins, an entrepreneur and business development and selling professional. I started my training around the ripe age of ten years old. My family raised us in a small town community in southwest Virginia. Little did I know that my standing in front of a big bathroom mirror selling shampoo or hairspray would lead to a career in sales. Sometimes I would grab a can of deodorant and tell the mirror why it was essential to wear it every day. I started giving product knowledge sessions in the mirror before I knew what a PK was! I spent hours practicing what it would be like to be on QVC and be one of those beautiful women selling twenty-four hours a day on a dedicated television channel.

Outside of babysitting and cleaning my dad's office, I took my first real paying job in 1997, when the internet world was emerging, at a telemarketing company in uptown Bluefield, WV. At the time, it was just a fun place to work and hang out with my friends before and after. Taking the job with my high school girlfriends as coworkers did not feel like a career decision. Little did I know I would develop skills in cold calling and rejection. Rebuttals and refusals started from scripts drafted by someone in a corporate office. The sales strategies for us young telemarketers were to follow the scripts provided and keep dialing, power through and endure the rejection, and aim to keep the target engaged for enough time to get them to agree to transfer to the closers. We were not the closers. We were the worker bees. We dialed and introduced products and made bets on how many minutes one of us could stay on the line before our customers hung up the phones abruptly.

The scripts are fuzzy memories, and I don't recall being exceptional at my job. Considering I arrived on the job with only the depth and skill gained by selling shampoo in the mirror, my first sales job proved helpful in developing hard and soft skills for the future: endurance, practicing rebuttals and refusals, patience, and listening. I recall finding the urge to compete on the leaderboard, and a competitive leader was born.

During my first retail sales job, I learned the importance of expertise in sales. I practiced controlling the sale, by gauging how many items to present for selections, and keeping the client's attention. One of my first significant closings on a retail floor happened with a sale of **$600** in ski apparel (in an American Eagle Outfitters location) to a family in Tuscaloosa, Alabama. My upbringing on the slopes of West Virginia ski resorts turned into expertise that day. But I wanted more of that feeling—that winning sensation!

My office and organizational skills began developing while living and working in New York City. During those years, I spent time in humility being other people's assistants; I gained the most knowledge of "what it takes." They say if you can make it in New York, you can make it anywhere. I don't think "I made it," but it definitely made me.

During a stint as a personal shopper in a boutique, I learned the art of merchandising products while catering to the local wealthy women's clientele. My mentor, Annette, taught me how to organize products for display, run a business, and increase sales by adding accessories. I developed sales pitch techniques and learned how to control the sale by understanding how customers reacted to suggestions in the clothing shop. With time, I began cold-calling customers regularly and became skilled at gauging the body language of my target contact. I continued overcoming the fear of picking up the phone and calling numbers at random.

By the time I started in the countertop industry (construction), I could implement all my previously learned skills and add new ones! As a result, I slowly transformed these skills into successful brand management and business development practices. I learned

- Territory routing
- Humility
- Integrity
- Public speaking

- Event planning

- The art of rebuttals and refusals

- The art of specification

- Knowing when it was time to move on to the next client

When I joined as a sales rep in a large distribution group, my techniques grew the branch sales by 67 percent in the first year. One manager, I recall, wasn't initially open to new sales strategies. He had his own ingrained experiences. Over time, however, and through perseverance, diligence, and a "proof is in the pudding" mentality, this manager eventually jumped on board with my implementing the change strategy. Together, we began shifting personnel into more appropriate roles. In addition, he allowed me more control over the department where I had the most expertise: natural stone and merchandising.

Now I run my own company: Rep Methods. The concept of Rep Methods began when a manager and I were struggling to train newer sales team members, both inside and outside. We often joked about my "methods," hence, my new company name, and how the manager wanted me to train all the salespeople into "order makers."

It's important to note that it took many years of cold-calling and learning customer nurturing to develop a "sixth sense" for selling. Some have referred to my intuition as "the stone whisperer." I've climbed mountains (literally). It took love and passion for a product from the earth to motivate me to keep going; my passion for educating and influencing generations after me encourages me to move forward. Ironically, it takes masochistic attitudes to push me toward breaking through the glass ceiling.

Why I wrote this book

My generation experienced learning with and without the aid of technology. While training people of all ages and genres, I have noticed several differences in terms of human interactions and learning methods in the generations following me. Some cannot make eye contact with their friends and are much less capable of walking into a business and instantly creating a relationship. Some have that ability but have ego issues. One twenty-five-year-old millennial required a "boot camp" style to get him confident in his innate abilities. Yes, he came with natural skills, and after breaking his pride a bit, he strived to soak up my experience. I've also trained older generations, and often technology and innovation defeat this group. Newer systems like CRMs often blow over more confident and historically booming careered salespeople. It's usually a challenge to break down an older salesperson's ego long enough to inspire changes in work habits. Overall, these experiences led me to embark on the journey to become a sales trainer. Customers across the mid-Atlantic requested I train their new hires. An organization where I was employed full time asked me to mentor new employees, so I began making notes about my skills every day for a year. I was hooked, knowing I could make a difference.

If you are willing to try and drop the ego and learn a new way, you can make changes for a healthier and happier career in sales. And that is the main reason for this book. I want you to find new methods, search for integrity and humility, and improve the overall customer service experience for your clients.

My goal is to help you <u>change</u>, improve, implement, and adapt a few simple processes which will increase your honesty, strengthen your work ethic, empower your networking abilities, and inspire you to expand your expertise and improve the business bottom line.

These stories and suggestions for navigating the world of sales and business development come from my heart.

What will you get out of this book?

This book to inspire change in strategy and create techniques of a new mindset for selling. *The Art of Selling* is about finding love and passion in a product or service that makes you happy. This book will inspire change in how you look at your customer targets, helping you to tackle a new approach to selling. I perhaps overemphasize new organizational techniques. It is my goal to provide experience and inspire change. After all, change is the only constant in our lives.

After reading these suggestions and implementing new habits into your workspace, you will develop stronger intuition, make your customers happier, create longer-lasting business relationships, increase your reliability, and become a more articulate salesperson. I can also promise you will close more deals, which will make you (and your boss) the happiest of all. So, after you finish this book, join us in conversations at @repmethods and www.repmethods.com. Let's discuss a seminar opportunity for your company's sales teams. I can't wait to meet you on the sales floor. Let's get started.

Section 1

Brand Management

Become the brand. Be the brand. Represent the brand.

In the age of social media, the word *brand* gets thrown around a lot, but how does one's brand affect sales and business development? Can a shift in focus to brand management increase sales? Can managing the brand better strengthen customer relationships?

In order to strengthen customer relationships, you need to know about the human ego.

The ego is defined as "one of three divisions of the psyche in psychoanalytic theory that serves as the organized conscious mediator between the person and reality, especially by functioning both in the perception of and adaptation to reality." [1] What this

---

[1]   Merriam-Webster.com, s.v. "ego (n)," accessed June 2023, https://www.merriam-webster.com/dictionary/ego.

means is the human ego is a human's perception of our self-worth. Therefore, the art of selling requires hitting various pieces of a customer's ego. We must dissect, target, aim, and hit those particular ego-driven areas to be successful.

Some customers require more of a relationship to keep their business. Some customers need to have an exclusivity factor to purchase. In marketing, target markets are invaluable to sales agents and marketing teams. In all sales environments (inside, outside, direct), we must know who our customer is and what it takes to keep them working with us in that moment, year, or lifetime and then make sure our brand supports our ideal client.

In the following chapters, we will outline three concepts for creating an optimal brand strategy and optimizing sales representation. To do this, you will need to hone skills in **etiquette** and organization while practicing **humility** and **integrity**.

Before you begin selling, you have to first clean up your act.

Chapter 1

BRAND MANAGEMENT ETIQUETTE

P roper business etiquette will improve your appearance and the representation of a brand. By implementing some changes, you will notice it's easier to activate sales and concentrate on the most critical selling parts: keeping your employer and clients happy, and making money.

Managing brand appearance

Managing brand appearance is one of the easiest ways to increase sales optimization and visibility, as it includes the simple tasks of grooming habits, apparel selection, and the appearance of company vehicles. The presentation of a brand (i.e., showroom appearance) can make or break a business relationship. For example, it's not the design of a logo; it's the consistency of the logo and its presentation throughout the package. Are you utilizing all possible resources for displaying the brand while you are selling? What can you change today to increase the brand's visibility?

Add company logos to all vehicles used for selling: This is normal if the vehicle is company-owned. But if you're using your personal car, ask the manager or owner if you can order branded magnets for all sides of the vehicle while in company use.

Vehicles used for the company: I once managed a sales associate whose car looked like a unicorn candy glitter bomb had exploded in every passenger seat. When we opened the fifth door hatch to access flooring samples, items fell to our feet, causing me to jump out of the way to avoid injury. This isn't appropriate or acceptable, ever. Company vehicles (or personal vehicles used for company purpose) must be organized and clean. If the car has company logos on it, you must maintain its appearance. As for the logos, keep them intact and free from scarring or excessive filth.

Grooming habits: A close friend of mine works in HR for a huge national brand. When I began writing my classes, she asked me if I wanted to alienate my audience by criticizing smoking and other personal habits that can affect sales. I told her this was a non-negotiable for me. As a smoker for twenty-five years, I had to follow extreme hygiene measures to ensure my lousy habit didn't affect my customers. I kept gum on me at all times and ensured I wasn't smoking within fifteen minutes of an appointment and that my apparel was free from smoke fragrances. While you may be offended, don't take this for granted: smoking is frowned upon more than ever.

Cover it up and keep it away from the clients.

As silly as it may seem, grooming habits matter. Men should keep their beards, mustaches, and facial hair tidy. Women should try to keep their hairstyles tactful, neat, and clean. Sure, on some days we've all been guilty of throwing our hair into a bun and walking out the door. But overall, you want to make sure your outward appearance reflects your brand's attributes and fits the mold the brand is trying to achieve. While some may call me "old-fashioned," this concept applies the old adage, we attract more bees with honey than with vinegar. We can create more attraction to ourselves and our expertise by looking the part and keeping the brand tidy.

Simple measures such as tucking in (or not) the company shirt, taking out body piercings, not wearing holey jeans, etc. Yes, we have the freedom of what we do to our bodies in the name of art, but that doesn't always mean it's right for the brand we are representing. I have a nose piercing and tattoos, but I make sure to take out the ring and cover up my tattoos when on the job. Again, I know I might be offending some people in my audience, but head-to-toe tattoos and facial piercings are 100 percent acceptable if you're selling tattoos and piercings, but may not be 100 percent acceptable when working behind the cosmetic counter at a retail store. All I ask is that we take those things into consideration for the brand we agree to represent. Companies can eliminate these issues by providing company shirts and logo apparel to keep the brand appearance consistent.

Communication: Sometimes it's not how you respond to clients, but when you respond, aka responsiveness, and the method in which you respond. In today's society, we've entered a world of non-human contact communication. Texting is the communication king for anyone under the age of fifty. However, email communication remains the leading medium of business communication in the twenty-first century. While many communications and transactions happen over text messages, at the very least, we should send larger files and product selection offers via email. With email, you need to follow up with specific clients to ensure they check their email.

Taking that extra follow-up step might seem excessive, but ensuring clients read your offers and submissions is worth the effort to win more sales. Also, it's important to factor in how easy it is to say no over email or text before choosing a method of communication (more to come on that later). An impersonal inquiry might warrant an easier no. Keep a recorded database, spreadsheet, or notation of all your customers who don't read emails. Taking a few minutes after a marketing blast to text these clients and alert them to your email will help you build results.

Use your email server's "read receipt" function: If you use this function, then immediately after sending a significant sale opportunity, you will know when the client opened and considered your offer. If you don't get a response in an appropriate amount of time (consider how long you let emails sit in your inbox without responding to the inquiry), then send a follow-email.

***Pro Tip**—check out a program like GMASS if you aren't working on Outlook. This program allows you to send individual emails without using bcc and contains tracking data so you can see the successes and failures of the communication. This helps you improve your email communication techniques, adapt, and ensure customers are receiving your messages.

Improve your response time: A rule of thumb in all industries is that emails should receive a response within twenty-four to forty-eight hours. If you can't respond in this time frame, a message should be sent to a customer explaining the delay and setting proper expectations for a timely response. Later, I talk about calendar blocking as an effective method of creating time. If you aren't responding to your clients within a good timeframe, you are losing sales, guaranteed.

Running late: Call or text if you are running late. It might be considered old-school to push the call, but it is the most respected method. Please consider your history of communication with this client before making a decision. Don't be selfish. Consider whether they called you, not texted you, to discuss the service, or if all communication has taken place via email. If this is the first time you will meet in person and don't have a communication history, it's best to call, as it is more personable and a better look for the brand.

Before you even go through the sales process with your next lead, take this opportunity to think about how you will communicate with them. What it takes to become a successful salesperson in communication is overcoming the urge to text or email and using your voice instead to communicate with your customers. Personalization tactics close sales.

Chapter 2

ORGANIZATION

Efficiency makes room for more profitability. More profitability is the reason companies hire me.

One way to increase efficiency is to get better organized. If a brand is a tree, **organization** is the tree's heart root. While my company can help you improve your lead capture and nurture, and we can teach you tricks to increase your sales numbers, we can't keep you organized. An effort to stay organized has to come from within you. Too many companies and employers don't hold employees accountable to stay organized. Managers brush this aside, calling those of us who nitpick about organization "micro-managers"; however, consider the aftereffects of a tornado for a moment. Picture what it's like for FEMA to help clean up after a significant storm. Picture the contents of homes spread far and wide. Insurance companies can only detail all the damages once the afflicted party records everything missing. An employee with no organizational skills resembles a house after a tornado; they won't be able to get as many sales and reap as many

7

benefits with sloppy organization. Let's compare homes after tornadoes to your current email situation. It might not be pretty.

Folder and email organization

Email organization: When I first entered the fashion workforce in New York City, I lucked out working for a seventy-year-old experienced vice president of sourcing. The man had difficulty typing but was a stickler for email organization. He would drop by my cubicle weekly to see if I'd cleaned out my inbox. Sonny instilled the practice of using Friday afternoons to file my emails away correctly. A clean inbox ensured I had completed all tasks, answered everything, and completed all follow-ups. Taking time to organize emails on Fridays allowed me to end the week with a quick numeric and handwritten Post-it with tasks for Monday the following week. At twenty-three years old, I initially got embarrassed if he caught me unorganized. Over time I started to expect these drop-ins, and within a few short months, I was an email filing master. I saved everything. While working as a product development manager for Ralph Lauren, they knew me for my little folders and subfolders in their email; I was like a beaver hoarding wood for his next dam build. The moral of this story is that no matter the profession, you always have time to organize. Look at your inbox and determine what folders and subfolders you could create to organize it.

Examples:

Client or account names as main folders, with projects as subfolders, making it easy to locate a specific conversation or topic chain.

In fashion we used seasons as the primary folders, then style numbers for the subfolders to keep all data properly organized.

With products, use the product as the main, but then include subfolders to easily identify product knowledge data, updates, or changes. You can even use the month as a subfolder to easily break down communications and locate chains from the past.

Proactive emailing: Sales and business development people who don't organize their emails miss sales opportunities. With a disorganized inbox, it's hard to have a proactive email strategy. Too many have a reactive email response strategy. I've watched salespeople waste time sitting in front of the screen and waiting for the leads and communications to come to them. Move away from a reactive mentality. Emails are to create leads and communicate with your clients, customers, and targets, not reactive responses! Let me clarify if you don't know what I mean by reactive response selling. Take a deep look at your email output. Are you responding to inquiries more than you're creating queries?

Take some time out of your work tomorrow to analyze your sent mailbox. Count how many emails you sent this week that were in response to an inquiry from a customer or a business and how many were an initiation of a conversation. If more than forty percent of your sent mails are in response to someone else's inquiry, then you are not a proactive salesperson, and you are currently in reactive-selling mode. More than seventy-five percent of your emails should prompt conversations, leads, and sales. With this singular shift in thinking, change is possible. How to implement this change is another strategy! Humans are creatures of habit. We are addicted to answering the inbox.

Manage share folders: In your business, are you required to photograph and sell inventory photos? Is that inventory under constant rotation? What methods are you using to organize your presentations for clients? To get organized, collect those photos in a shared folder catalog. Spending a little time to do this at the beginning or end of the week makes the inner week workflow move faster. In the surfaces industry, selling wholesale, we must take photos of arriving inventory and then text, email, and blast advertisements to our customers, not to mention keeping price lists, product facts, forms, spreadsheets, and general documents organized. What if you are a service? Do you need to qualify your work for your clients? Using a set shared folder for uploading job photos is essential to qualify your brand. Get a system in place and create time to keep it clean.

Keeping the share folder system organized is the challenging part, but as many salespeople are moving from various devices, the system you choose needs to be maintained so you can find data easily, quickly, and spontaneously when working with a client.

I used the following organization system when I was an account manager selling to hundreds of clients:

Primary folders per product and annual sub folders so I could hold onto previous years' data and refer back when necessary. Within each product, I had separate pricing folders for spreadsheets and price lists. Then I had flyers or advertising data folders to quickly pull up email and advertising items. Photo folders are common for all salespeople, as we must keep project data and history photos in order to sell more stuff! Imagine if we put everything into the photo folder and simply left it in bulk form. We would never find anything when we needed it.

I found it helpful to create subfolders to make presentations of particular groups or categories so I could pull those up when a question on that category emerged and use the photos for my sales explanation!

It's easy to talk about doing the organization, but we also have to schedule and set aside time in order to keep this organized. I suggest making a reoccurring monthly slot on your calendar to take an hour and update your organization.

Time management

Time management is a critical organizational tactic for outside salespeople in particular. You must optimize appointments and scheduling. Technology is helpful in

11

today's process for calendar and time management. If your organization uses a CRM, it's more important than ever to use this service for planning and logging how you spend time on the job. Start slowly. Follow the tips below, set time aside daily, and get comfortable putting all personal and professional appointments in a calendar system. Do you deal with contractors who start working at the crack of dawn? Are you presenting to interior designers who may have to work until 10 p.m. and can only come to the office at 10 a.m.?

You must be willing to organize your schedule according to the availability of your clients. Too often I encounter salespeople who work the schedule according to their own personal needs and refuse to create opportunities that better fit the customer's needs. The keywords here: *create opportunities*. People have kids and families and religious or volunteer obligations, so you need to get creative in making yourself available. One of my training pet peeves is someone who says, "I don't have time." The truth is they aren't making the time and creating those opportunities. If you find yourself in a position where you aren't willing to better accommodate the customer's schedule, you might be in the wrong position in the company.

Use a planner: I advise any new outside sales or account representative to start their work by utilizing a planner, journal, notebook, or a similar item for documenting day-to-day notes, sales opportunities, names, and conversation notations with a physical ink pen or pencil. If you're starting fresh or kicking habits, the traditional fifty-two-week planner is the best option before transitioning to a best practices method in CRM systems. Using this traditional handwritten planner will get you into the routine of jotting down your daily schedule. If you want to drive more sales into the business, create a plan and a time for cold calling and capturing leads.

Use calendar blocking: Have you ever heard of calendar blocking? This is when you set time blocks on the calendar to perform a certain task and use technology to remind you to stay organized. Having these scheduled blocks helps to keep anxiety at bay. For example, block time for follow-up emails, time for organization, and time for making calls. Take a break from the sales floor and make those calls. You and your team can enjoy the benefits of the freedom to focus on one specific task during that window. It's not just about getting work done during business hours; it's also about giving you and your teammates peace of mind. If you are in a busy showroom and never seem to find the time for X, then this is when you need to negotiate with a superior or another employee to free up some time for these blocks in a quiet zone.

If you work on the road, make sure you set a time block for follow-up communication. Typically, I urge the reps I am training to finish their appointments by 3:30 p.m. each day so they can use the rest of the afternoon to stop in a quiet place and complete the necessary CRM data entry and or complete the follow-up emails and offers based on the interactions which occurred.

*Pro tip—if you use a CRM for data entry daily, set aside a time block each day to do your data entry. This will make it easier to execute your follow-up. As you enter the notes from each visit, you will remember what you need to send! It's that simple! Kill two birds with one stone: keep track of the notes from the day and help yourself to expedite follow-up communication.

If you work on the road, like I did for most of my career, try planning your week at least one, if not two, weeks in advance. If you wait until Monday to plan your week, you are wasting the business's precious time and are already behind the ball. If you have a plan in place, when Monday rolls around after the weekend, you won't have to think about what to do and waste time, you simply execute what you already planned. Preparing a plan in advance based on the encounters from the previous week ensures I don't forget those precious conversations and interactions from the week prior. Sometimes I request that newcomers purchase a thirty-day desk calendar so we can work on planning and routing in bimonthly segments. Retail showroom staff often get locked behind the computer when not dealing with a client. The calendar blocking method is a successful way to create time to handle those pesky follow-up, organization, and lead-generation tasks.

Routing and mapping: If you're driving most of the day, take some time to find a map routing tool. Often those professional CRMs come equipped with one. If you don't have access to a CRM system, get comfortable using tools like Google Maps. Save your repeated routes to help you execute time management and efficiency.

Personal boundaries and time management: Our personal schedules somehow become a second-tier priority when we are an active salesperson. Remember, you must schedule time for mental release. Whether it's the gym, professional therapy, or fun outdoors with your fur babies, make sure to schedule that time and do it!

Ensure your personal calendar can be "seen" in your professional calendar version and vice versa. This way, you will schedule yourself around both personal and professional commitments. Avoid scheduling meetings outside of work hours and establish boundaries.

Chapter 3

HUMILITY AND INTEGRITY

It doesn't matter if you sell apparel, flooring, car parts, hair products, food and wine, or granite—every salesperson and every brand requires **humility** and **integrity** to sustain and create a business while representing a brand. As I mentioned in the intro, I don't intend to give you a "get rich quick" scheme. I offer zero promises for excessive financial gain. What I do promise is sustainability and longevity in a sales career. The Rep Methods way and my personal beliefs follow integrity and humility, demonstrating the path to more profitable and long-term sales.

In outside sales, retail, and business development: The first six months begin with introductions into the market and creating a structure. Once you have done that, it's time to develop key relationships. This requires both humility and integrity. Both critical etiquettes are about remaining important to your client. Do yourself a favor and become the reliable resource they contact in a pinch. As you grow in your career, please take care to do the research before answering, staying humble enough to know you don't know everything. Keep the integrity of your efforts clear to the client by demonstrating your loyalty.

- Make time for each client and alert them in advance of your service.

- Let them know you intend to focus on them and provide superior service.

- Remain compassionate of their needs, which means knowing when to back off a sale even when you want to attack and keep hounding.

The repeated effort to call, visit, follow up, and show up overtime demonstrates a loyalty and integrity that all customers find irresistible. It appeals to the client's ego and helps to establish a relationship.

In direct selling: There is no time to develop a relationship with the customer. Instead, it's all about closing the sale quickly. Integrity and humility may seem counterproductive in this aggressive selling strategy; however, they will also result in stronger post-sale foundations and help expedite the sales process if appropriately executed. During this high-pressure, high-turnover field, it's your job to sell the client something they didn't know they needed. So how can you stay humble and keep integrity in the process? The best-case scenario is to remain honest with as much information as possible. If you want to stay happy and healthy in this career, using cheap and sneaky tactics to close a deal might win you a sale, but what will the guilt do to you later?

Direct selling with integrity leads to more effective selling longer term. If you sell knives in a neighborhood, do you expect to sell to one or all the houses? If you don't show integrity, word will spread and you will lose all the sales in the neighborhood. It benefits you to create an exceptional experience from the get-go. Will the honest and complete sale turn into other sales using proper post-sale foundations? Don't plan on closing one deal; work to close one hundred instead.

Lead Management

L ead management involves capturing leads, qualifying your leads by identifying products to sell,
nurturing the lead into a sale, and furthering an
ongoing customer relationship. In layman's terms:
finding customers, approaching the sale correctly,
and cultivating relationships for future sales.

A near-miss turned into a success—a story of lead management

When I was working with a company in Virginia, I got
a panicked call from a manufacturer's representative
of a quartz product line that we distributed. The
representative was upset, having received several
emails and phone calls from a client in the New York
market stating they hadn't received a response to
their online inquiry. The manufacturer was alarmed
because the customer claimed they had inquired
through our websites. Online leads are less common

than those from traditional local customers. Stepping in, I did some digging and asked around the office to see if anyone had taken any emails or phone calls from this client. The lead had been passed to a newer quartz account manager and, unfortunately, the emails and phone calls went unanswered.

The client had requested four samples and distribution information on a newer color. These types of simple sample inquiries often dry out, and we may never hear from the client again, but using diligent follow-up skills, we turned this inquiry into a **$10,000** sale for the location.

The process that closed the deal: After stepping in, I telephoned the client within ten minutes of hearing about the communication delay. I apologized to the client for any communication mishaps. She explained her project required X slabs of material, and her contractor would be ready to order as soon as she approved the samples. The next day, my team overnighted the samples to the client in New York, and I sent her a tracking number. I followed up through a text three days later to ensure she had received the samples. She confirmed by reply. Next, we arranged a consultation call to discuss the timeline for her order. I scheduled follow-up dates on my calendar to ensure I wouldn't forget.

Unfortunately, we only had eight slabs of this material in that area, and she needed more. But I used that to my advantage, telling her that if she wanted to secure the material for her contractor, we would happily take a deposit to lock in her slabs. The client paid for the material that day to avoid losing the slabs. Our branch secured a sale. The final step for the salesperson was coordinating with logistics to ship material up to her contractor.

What action did it take to close a sale from an online sample request? Action and lead conversion start with urgency in completing that first phone call to the client. After some soft-hearted understanding of her project's urgency, a few diligent motions to answer her needs, and many follow-ups, I closed the sale.

This story example covers the entire process from lead to sale. It took phone calls and texts over the next few weeks to determine a timeline and review the approval of the samples, but with several follow-ups, this random web inquiry lead brought a nice marginal sale for the month.

This shows that some leads may appear unimportant on the surface, but you need to treat them with that same attitude of importance as you do with important leads! Handling leads is a priority! It's how salespeople win customers, loyalty, and close deals!

Chapter 4

LEAD CAPTURE AND QUALIFYING SALES

When it comes to capturing leads, we can be our own worst enemy in the field. Yes, we might face rejection, and yes, we might be uncomfortable at first and awkward! However, the more we grow our network, the easier it will become to capture leads and qualify them for sales and/or new business relationships.

Lead capture and qualification skills include cold calling, identifying target accounts using networking and research, and turning those cold leads into warm accounts. To better understand your direct involvement in the lead capture and qualification processes, let's document how leads are generated in your organization.

Identifying target accounts using networking and researching

Whether you are in a business-to-business or business-to-consumer model, you must create opportunities to interact and then record that information (the best way is using a CRM).

You want to create opportunities with your target clients. Think of lead capture as an octopus. Those eight tentacles are a form of collecting leads and customers. Each arm of the octopus is a method to "grab" new business. Each one of these tentacles can represent a marketing medium for direct sales, such as internet, TV, radio, social media, word of mouth, networking, print ads, or trade shows.

So with wholesale for business development, each one of the arms can identify all the networking and research methods we should use to connect with our target audience, such as specific industry groups for networking, shared data websites, types of continuing education programs, trade shows, etc.

If you want to explore this concept, take a few minutes to draw a circle on the paper, draw eight lines from the circle, and write out how your business is currently receiving its leads. If you have purchased the workbook designed to pair with this book, you have some blank octopus charts to practice this. Diagramming will be helpful if you are new to the company, or perhaps you are also the business owner and reading this book to rebuild a sales team. The inside of the circle isn't simply your business name, but the target customer you need to reach. Each one of these tentacles needs to extend from where you expect to capture your customer, just like an octopus catches its prey in the wild. Make sense? Here is an example.

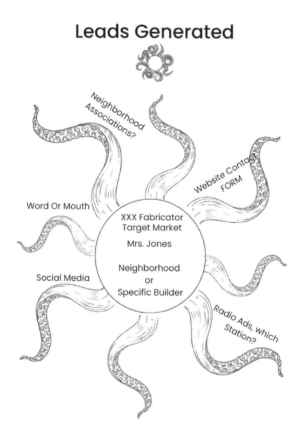

Leads Generated

Neighborhood Associations?

Website Contact FORM

Word Or Mouth

XXX Fabricator
Target Market

Mrs. Jones

Neighborhood
or
Specific Builder

Social Media

Radio Ads, which Station?

Use this one, or look in your workbooks for more blank versions to try on your own.

27

Target Clients

Okay, wholesalers, do you need to network more and open the possibilities to create new leads and accounts? Look closely at the octopus diagram once again. Now, consider what you sell; I'm serious, think wholeheartedly about the product, followed by the ideal retail, then get bigger and start thinking about the industry, and then go even bigger by considering adjacent industries. WOW, the potential for leads just expanded tenfold!

Target Client Networking

ONLINE Forums??

Builder Associations

BNI Groups?

Contracters & Remodelers Tile Showrooms

National Construction Groups?

PRODUCT: **Setting Adhesives for Stone**

TIle Setters (obvious)

Kitchen & Bath Associations?

Real Estate Groups?

Are you **networking** using all the right possibilities to reach your customer? What about industry-adjacent associations? Consider using all your tools in your networking "octopus' chart" to start identifying new leads for your business. Also, keep in mind, research is a more than one-size-fits all approach. The more we research who we are targeting, the stronger the leads we will generate, allowing us to strategically narrow our approach to the larger markets and industries.

Examples of experienced direct sales agents working in **lead capture networking** are mortgage brokers and real estate agents. These salespeople are key experts to follow. They know how to network in various segments outside their traditional network, creating client circles. BNI groups are excellent places to network for direct sellers. These groups encourage doing business within the group first!

Whether you are inside or outside sales, if you need help, start with the basics. Identify a general service area you wish to establish. Is there a particular census category (zip code, demographic, industry, sector) you want to target? Can you break these categories down further? Try.

Networking can be challenging! Trust me, I understand the importance of selecting the best groups to spend your time with! We only have so much time to spare in life, so we need to select the best two, three, or four groups to participate in. If I can impart one or two techniques to open your eyes and find that broader audience, then I've done my job. Recently I moved into networking with the National Association of Women in Construction, a group outside my comfort zone, but philanthropically, they identify and execute events more alongside my goals and aspirations. This group intimidated me at first because I wasn't sure I belonged. I didn't work in construction; I work construction adjacent! I have worked in product specification on commercial projects and luxury residential for many years, but not actually on their side of the project.

But in researching new networking groups, I found this group focused on youth education and the development of future generations, moving them toward jobs in trade. NAWIC also hosts a camp every year for middle schoolers to learn about the industry, letting campers participate in various trade careers during their week camp, gaining experience and knowledge and planting those future seeds of passion. Youth education for trade is something we are missing in my direct industry of surfaces. So in finding this adjacent group, I found someone to mentor me and nurture my exploration into this new path I want for my career in the future. This adjacent network will not only expand my local but also my national community. It isn't just about new mentorship; potential sales may come from this new group too! I host seminars and promote training, so these new networks just gave me a whole new branch of connector groups and opportunities to spread my messages.

As you can see capturing leads starts with a variety of attack methods. While many come from the marketing efforts of an organization, you can work diligently to capture the leads and then listen closely to the target clients to find out how you will qualify your products into a sale for them. As with the initial story of the email inquiry for samples, this was an example of low-hanging fruit! Since the client had identified and told us exactly which product she wanted, we didn't have to qualify the client for a specific product; however, it was necessary we move her into the sale and create proactive efforts to push the lead into the selling process. It's really as simple as listening, interpreting, and mind-reading our targets, right? Just kidding! We aren't mind readers, but we do have to use those instincts, that emotional intelligence, to let the clients guide us into the qualified sale.

Cold calling

Cold calling means picking up the *phone* and calling or *walking into a customer's home or business location* with your product or service without them having reached out. Yes, generation next, I'm talking about physically using the phone to make a call, not a text, or physically going to their place, not sending an email. Cold calling doesn't have to be a terrifying situation. But don't worry, if that's how you feel, you are not alone! Between you and me, warm calls are more manageable and less stressful. After all, generally, cold calls interrupt someone's day; therefore, effective cold calling requires certain techniques.

Once I was training a young salesperson with a mild-mannered, soft-hearted personality who only had a few years of experience in product knowledge and inside sales. They were assigned a territory as an outside wholesale representative and were required to market our brand as a representative to the retail customer. They were absolutely scared to death to cold-call the retail customers. As we moved into training, I pushed them toward a few cold calls, and I could tell they became nervous, sweating bullets as we pulled up in the parking lot.

Typically, when I train, I lead by example and encourage them to practice following my example. Over time, trainees learn to endure the rejection on their own. Over three months, I introduced him to the process of walking into a company unannounced (retail operations) and introducing ourselves and our products. He observed me finding the decision-maker and engaging in conversation. Most of the time we were in cities where I had zero experience or connection, and the young man was amazed I could turn a cold-call, walk-in visit into an hour-long meeting with follow-up planned and presentations on the books. Learning by example, he began to take the lead and his fear of failure began to fade. With *practice, listening,* and *observation,* he improved and became more comfortable with the process!

Limbic resonance—the ideal cold-call outcome: Recently, I read an outstanding leadership book called *Primal Leadership* that describes the concept of limbic resonance. The book defines *limbic resonance* as "a symphony of mutual exchange and internal adaptation, whereby two people harmonize their emotional state." By definition, this classic business book encapsulates what salespeople must achieve using the telephone, entering that doorway, or meeting face-to-face. We are looking to use our triage of **self-awareness, self-management**, and **empathy** within one minute, five minutes, ten minutes, or an hour of interpersonal communication. When we cold-call, we want to use **chameleoning** (explained later) and our network knowledge to turn these cold calls into warm leads. Deciding the method of approach will depend upon the business category, personnel structure, and receptiveness to walk-in traffic.

Try to gauge the feeling in your gut, the response from the company. Once you learn to "read the room," your success rate will increase with ample practice every week. What is the ultimate goal of your cold calls? Is it the recognition of a brand? Are you a direct seller who has to perform cold calls on a daily basis? Are you a software sales rep or sales experience rep whereby each day you are interacting with new team players and/or "cold calling" companies regularly to pitch a product?

Finding a connection. During a cold call, finding a connection is key. When we break down an obstacle by finding a connection with a lead, we change a cold call into a **warm lead**. Therefore, establishing a *name, project, connection, family relationship, religious connection, resemblance, history, friendship, college drinking story, or other connection* before making a call will increase the likelihood that the call will last longer than thirty seconds. With today's online resources, doing research through companies like LinkedIn, or via social media, makes connecting cold leads to warm calls easier than ever before. This straightforward strategy increases chances for success by exponential results.

One of my fondest memories of using my connections to convert an entire territory from cold to warm is the story of a special person in Atlanta, GA: Mr. Brad Hanner. If you are from Atlanta and have worked in design, construction, or remodeling in this market, you know Brad! He is the "Mr. Connection" networking genius in Atlanta's construction, remodeling, and building and interior design world. To further the importance of this market, Atlanta is the architecture and design capital of the south. I met Brad through a distributor while contracting for an Italian manufacturer. Meeting Brad changed my networking game in this city.

Companies I couldn't even get past the gatekeeper with now seemingly opened their doors and let me right in! My first mentor, Phil Devore (I'll tell you his story in the next chapter), told me many times how difficult Atlanta can be to master and break through. But Brad taught me how to open all the doors. So what is Brad's magic, and do you need magic? No, you don't need magic; you need to find the people who already have magic established. Trust me, they exist, which is precisely why we network.

Walk-in method: If initial telephone calls have gone unreturned and emails requesting appointments are unanswered, try the walk-in method. This can help you break through a barrier of non-response and gain their attention. Sometimes dropping off a physical business card and establishing a general interest in scheduling further contact is all it takes to break that barrier.

When I walk in, upon reaching the receptionist, I introduce myself, stating, "Good morning. My name is Alison. I apologize for any inconvenience, but I hoped to request a brief five-minute conversation with *X*. Would it be possible for you to verify if they are available to speak with me?" If the walk-in method is unsuccessful, give the effort a break for a few months and set a time to follow up again later in the year. The contact gap will not go unnoticed.

Getting past a notorious gatekeeper: Gatekeepers are lovely people assigned to "hold down the fort" in the front of a business. In construction and building companies, these various personnel are hired to make our lives miserable. All industries have "gatekeepers." If you sell hospital equipment, the surgeon's assistant is a gatekeeper; if you sell office supplies, the receptionist is the gatekeeper; etc. Some days the gatekeeper's entire purpose is to ensure you stay on your side of the telephone line, desk, door, or entry. I was intimidated by a few of these specially trained forces for many years, but I learned to overcome that fear through **warm call** techniques!

One of my favorite techniques to move past a gatekeeper is to bring snacks. This may seem cliché; however, finding out what makes a gatekeeper's sweet tooth sing is considered the low-hanging fruit of getting on the other side of that reception desk.

Another method is "over-communicating" with the gatekeeper well in advance of your non-appointment. Being annoying works sometimes. In some cases, by over-contacting, eventually, we wear them down and get let in.

I have learned that if I walk in cold to a gatekeeper with no advance notice, I am sure to be shut down and denied entry. Ironically, if I place that power back into the hands of the gatekeeper instead of trying to take away their authority, I smooth right on by every time. You also want to make the gatekeeper feel as though you see value in their importance. In order to do this, we must take the time to call in advance, even if that means calling them while sitting outside in the parking lot. Take a moment to put the power back into this gatekeeper's hands by appealing to their ego. Let them know you want to check in with them before coming by to see what time would work today. Make sure they know how much you need their help and approval to make this visit worthwhile. Find that resource or connection to bring them over to your side of the fence by empowering the gatekeeper in your success or failure for the day. Now, they don't need to know that you are going to make this meeting happen regardless and with or without them, right? Nope, but you appeal to their ego and act as though you need their help to make it happen.

I am still a little shaken at the memories of a couple of gatekeepers from my past travels. On one journey through an old territory, I recall hearing we were going to visit and call upon one of these notorious businesses without an appointment. I quickly made a few phone calls to some old contacts and friends from the car. I needed to save us both from the vicious beating I feared lay on the other side of that glass door. With one phone call, I learned she had retired, and it became safe to cross the threshold. Ironically, as we entered the semi–cold call, the business owner passed through, and since I had a history of working with the business, he recognized me. I couldn't have asked for a better cold-to-warm opportunity. Since I was traveling with a young representative, our current cold call turned warm through that recognition and led to a successful visit. It's funny how things change as we progress in our careers. The story's moral is to always establish a connection before making a connection. It makes business development and sales warmer, more effortless, and our "limbic tangos" smoother.

Just like in the cold-call process, we need to use our triage of **self-awareness**, **self-management**, and **empathy** so the client can send us clues about what we will sell them. If they aren't giving up that information quickly, it's our job to ask probing questions to draw the client into qualified responses. There is a good chance you are already doing this in your day-to-day without even knowing you're qualifying them.

Do you have a questionnaire you start off with over the phone or in person? How do you identify their needs and eliminate products that will not work for the customer? Before you begin the pitch, you need to identify what you can eliminate from the sale process right off the bat. This is the act of qualifying the lead.

Some example lead qualification questions:

- What brings you in today?
- How did you hear about us?
- Have you shopped with anyone else yet?
- What problem are you experiencing?

- Are there two items you are deciding between? Let's discuss those.

- Have you purchased this before?

- What worked for you last time? What didn't?

- What budget do we have to work with?

At this point, you are approaching the customer nurture process. We have enabled the client to provide us with all the information we need to make a sale. But, before we move on, I wanted to highlight some variations in technique required depending on target market and product category. As I mentioned above, I've worked both in commercial construction and luxury residential product specifications. Luxury customers can be harder to network with. Don't give up, and recognize the more luxurious the customer or the more lucrative the project, the more research will be required to reach that audience. In those situations, an outside sales rep must troll deep inside the target client's online profile to find out as much as possible before attempting cold or warm calls. In another role in my career, I felt more like an FBI investigator than a self-described architectural and design marketing agent. The high-end luxury manufacturer requested we move about the continent serving distributor territories. We visited a region for a week or two at a time, made appointments to discuss projects, showcase products, and demand attention for a brand. These accounts are not the type of business where a person can walk in "cold" and expect to have a meeting. To succeed, we needed to **research** the critical decision-maker far in advance of a cold call and try to use **networking** skills to turn the cold call into a warm lead. These types of clients need more than lead qualifications; they need you to have done your research well before the appointment. This type of client expects you to walk in the door with a known solution without knowing the problem. Expertise is of the up-most importance in working with luxury and multi-million dollar project segments. If you are not quite to this level, don't be afraid to partner up with someone who has the experience you need to guide you into proper product qualifications and other techniques. In the next chapter, we will discuss expertise and how to get there from here.

**A note to my outside specification teams: sometimes for proper networking, we must be prepared to use our time management and schedule appointments months in advance. In one of my classes, "The Art of Specification," I go into detail about utilizing continuing education programs, architectural library visits, and project research to connect my research to lead capture in the construction industry. As this is a complicated subject, check out the topic and class on our website: www.repmethods.com/onlinecourses.

Chapter 5

LEAD AND CUSTOMER NURTURE

To become the customers' go-to person, you need to first nurture leads into clients, then continue to nurture the client to build foundations for future sales. If you want to nurture the lead, you need to become an expert.

Expert

Who decides when we have the right to call ourselves a "real-life subject matter expert"? To become an expert, you need the drive, practice, love, and passion to pursue learning all you can in your chosen field. But you still may question yourself. I often ask, "Who am I to decide that I've achieved such a status?" Let's look at an example of a fantastic expert in his field.

Aaron Franklin started his Franklin Barbecue business in 2009. If you get in the doors today, prepare to wait several hours to grab a seat. Yes, his company is doing that well. Yet he lost his business entirely in 2017 because of a fire. Regardless of the setback, he rebuilt and continued on his path to success, exemplifying his expertise. Aaron Franklin began setting a new standard for barbecue. He was the first barbecue chef to win a James Beard Award. By 2013, his BBQ business hit the charts in the local publication's "50 Best BBQ Joints." In 2012, Anthony Bourdain visited him for one of his *No Reservations* episodes, but a PBS television series in 2013 earned him true fame and showcased his expertise.

Aaron didn't hide his barbecue strategy. He designed his new series, *BBQ with Franklin*, to showcase his craft and explain his process for barbecue. He revealed all his secrets. Years of practice are depicted on the screen for the public to view. Anyone with a grill could just as easily copy what Aaron was doing and never have to visit his restaurant, for there he was telling all those professional secrets and getting more famous by the second. It didn't hurt that this time in America was a food boom, and we started getting obsessed with "famous restaurants." If you watch the PBS series, Aaron talks about having mentors and learning about his methods for barbecue. He didn't simply wake up one Sunday morning and say, "I'm going to become a BBQ expert and have the best barbecue brisket in Texas." Nope, **Aaron had to study, work, develop, practice, and fall in love with his craft.** To do this, he first found a mentor to follow.

Mentorship: Getting a mentor is the best way to become an expert in your field. Find someone who can provide you with value, someone you want to follow, listen to, and grow with. In our era, you may be tempted to do this virtually. After all, we live in a different world now with TikTok, podcasts, Instagram Reels, and feed after feed after feed. Most of us get our knowledge from YouTube or these video content channels. But I suggest you find a live human, not just someone on a video. Find someone in your business community who inspires you to do more, encourages you to be better, and can teach you the ways of the industry.

My first commercial mentor was Phil Devore from Birmingham, AL. Phil would answer my phone calls and convince the company we worked for to allow him to visit Virginia and work with me a few days every few months. Each time he arrived in Virginia, he had pre-scheduled a set of "lunch and learns" with local architect firms. Phil scheduled the day for us each time, so all I had to do was show up. And I was happy to show up, watch, listen, and learn as he showed me the ropes of teaching people who are way more intelligent than we are about designing a product or service installation. Each time I learned how he connected with the audience. Phil would allow me to be his "Vanna White." If you are born after 1989, you need to Google who she is, but for those of us from earlier eras, we know her as the queen of Wheel of Fortune "show and tell." I began my career in commercial specifications by showing and telling while Phil talked.

Within my career, I've been a mentor and a mentee. Some people knew they were my mentor, and some didn't need to. The secret is to find a person with a key to a door you want to open and follow them through the door to the other side of your career hurdle. Stay humble enough to know those mentor opportunities exist at all levels.

Love: Another key element in developing expertise is love. While I worked with a medium-sized distribution group, the corporate executives pushed us to read a book by Steve Farber called *The Radical Leap*. In this book, the characters lead us down a rabbit hole of personal mystery, all while implementing the strategy that you must *love* what you do. If we could all live on vacation and make money, we'd opt for the vacation life. But what if you could find passion and love for at least a portion of what you do? For me, it's in the stone. Once I started traveling to Italy and visiting quarries, my fascination with this beast of nature exploded inside me. I wanted to know more and more and more, and it's one of those subject matters where you can never know it all, but it's inspiring to try. Find love for the product and a passion for learning every day.

Practice: As they say, practice makes perfect. There is no time limit on when we cross a threshold of expertise, but one day you get to write those words out on a post or blog. Someone will introduce you as a subject expert, and you will have arrived.

Networking now and in the future: A couple of easy and free ways to become an expert are by networking and taking part in continuing education. Experts must stay up to date with their education. How will we be networking in the Metaverse in the future? Many of us are already networking online locally or nationally. But what about in person? Despite technological progress, physically attending events, networking, and introducing oneself and one's brand remains an essential sales tactic that will never fade. As a salesperson, you must embrace swallowing your pride, tuck your ego, and attend peer meetings in person. Holy cow, that's magical! When meeting in Zoom rooms or Metaverse meeting spaces, it's easy to not pay attention to others. How will we engage without human connection? I'm no psychologist. Call me old-fashioned but get your butt to the local events and meet the people. The last part I want to impart about networking and engaging in networking events is how your peers perceive you. Wine, cheese, and handshakes at events allow you to learn from others, represent your brand, and expand your network in your community. It also allows you to become recognizable in your community. Networking and exhibiting our expertise is how we become **"the first call."** You become the face in the memory banks of your peers as the one who will have the answer.

Continuing Education: Use those local networking opportunities to find continuing education opportunities, expanding your knowledge and honing your craft. Over time, salespeople need "rounding out." For instance, when I started in countertops, I knew nothing about remodeling a house. I was a city girl down from New York City who had some expertise in cashmere sweaters, but certainly no knowledge about types of drywall. Engaging in the various industry community groups and participating in the continuing education programs available to me (for free typically), I began to round out my knowledge of the industry. Not only that, but I also gathered experience of how others perform the same methods. Little did I know I would be providing nearly one thousand CEUs in person over the next few years. The skills and experience I gained from seeing successful (and not-so-successful) event execution prepared me to move forward and enabled me to smoothly move into the commercial and luxury residential market with certified designers and architects as my target audience.

How to nurture leads

Now that you're a subject-matter expert, you can get your lead's attention, and from there, you need to nurture that lead.

Observation: To nurture leads, you must quickly **observe** your surroundings, as you need to read those emotional cues and eyeball customer details. This tactic is crucial for direct sellers in setting up the entire selling process. Whenever you walk into a client's home, look at your surroundings and immediately process "the style" of the customer. This will help you tailor your style of selling.

Let's look at an example. If you're selling patio awnings and they're a warm lead, as they requested you come over, when you walk into a home, notice where the outdoor exits are near the living spaces. Do the clients have tables and chairs for eating meals outside? Can you collect any **observations** to produce upselling opportunities? Is the client "aging in place" (a client who has decided to live in their forever home and won't be moving anytime soon or ever) and a candidate for a mechanized version of the awning? These clients are willing to spend more on upgrades for items that guarantee a better quality of life. Finding one of these clients is a great way to observe what problems you can solve for them with your upgrades and add-ons and justify the additional financial investment as an incentive. The client may work from home and so may be interested in outdoor walls, making it more like adding an extra room onto the house.

Also, observe opportunities to better connect with a client. If they have various paintings on their walls, you could bring up your passion for painting and experiences visiting museums around the country. Do they happen to have excessive football memorabilia, which could help you start a conversation and break the icy cold barrier?

Use the concept of chameleoning: If all else fails, make yourself look, talk, eat, and be more like your customer so they like you better. This is called chameleoning. This strange word is a self-preservation technique and a great way to nurture leads into sales. Some may consider it transactional, and some may consider it a negative personality trait. However, in sales and business development, this characteristic demonstrates empathy. Maggie Zhou quotes clinical psychologist Mary Spillane: "Being able to adapt to a situation and meet the needs of that situation means you are more likely to succeed."[2] This is an effective tool for social influence that can improve relationship management and closing skills, ultimately leading to more and better sales. Let's walk through an example.

Have you experienced attending a business luncheon? Have you heard the advice, "Order the same entrée as your host"? Following this chameleon technique ensures you both eat within a specific price point. As a result, neither of you will order anything out of the approved price range. It also helps to set the pace of the meal. If you are both eating the same meal, you can ensure to "pace yourself" through the conversation and keep your client comfortable and on their timeline.

When I started working for the Italian family, they decided we would train at the Verona, Italy, office for several weeks. I was deathly afraid I wouldn't fit in. I spoke a little Italian from my exchange student days, but I wanted desperately to fit in and nurture this employment relationship. I am a slightly overweight American blonde from Virginia with a New York accent and a bold attitude. The only part of me that I thought would be accepted was my love for cigarettes

---

2   Maggie Zhou, "Is 'Chameleoning' Subconsciously Impacting Your Social Life?," Refinery29, updated March 10, 2022, https://www.refinery29.com/en-gb/chameleon-effect.

and red wine. I wasn't selling a product; I was selling myself. Long story short, I did my best to study the apparel and get my language skills up to par and chameleon'd myself to fit in as best as possible. Before the trip I began to brush up on my old Italian skills. I downloaded apps to help me practice communication and accent. I had to tone down some of my "Americana" for the board room by staying quiet and monitoring how the employees corresponded with the big boss. Before heading to train for several weeks, I had a previous mentor help me plan my outfits to ensure I would blend into the European culture. All humans can be chameleons. This technique doesn't mean being "fake" or two-faced; it's more about blending in and cooperating with culture norms, whether that's the culture of a company or country. It's easier said than done and takes practice.

To effectively chameleon, you need to learn emotional intelligence and empathy. It doesn't have to be an innate gift. Just begin researching and learning to read body language. Can you recognize cues when it's time to change the subject? Should you introduce a closing action question or listen and stop talking? In my online courses, particularly the course on in-home/direct sales, I refer to our personalities as either a mouse or an elephant. Which one are you? In business-to-business or business-to-consumer models, recognize how your tone can change the conversation and keep a close eye on when you cross from eagerness about the exchange to conversation domination. Understanding the personality quirks of your client will help you improve conversations.

Many of us have outgoing, bombastic, and sometimes over-bearing personalities. Humbly, I admit it was challenging to take on a more restrained tone. If any of my former coworkers read this section, there will be smiles remembering how loud I am in person. I'm not afraid to admit faults, and this was one of mine, but over the years, I learned how to tone it down, which was necessary. The art of reading a room, anticipating each personality upon introduction, is a skill! Learning how to be quiet and listen is a good start.

Qualifying the brand: Let's look at how brand qualifying works to nurture leads.

Brand qualifying requires you to be an expert. Get comfortable with being an "expert" even if you lack years of experience. If you study product knowledge, stay in tune with trends, and know the competition's selling angles, you are well on your way to being that "expert" in the field.

When working in a retail clothing shop, we sold cashmere sweaters, cardigans, and other apparel with a starting price of over **$500.00** each. The customers, typically women or husbands, were all repeat clients. The store owner had a reputation for servicing a luxury clientele. As a salesperson, I needed to become familiar with yarns, fiber contents, wash care, wear instructions, and iron ability. In addition, I needed to qualify each brand sold by demonstrating and discussing their exceptional quality.

When interacting with repeat customers, conversations revolved around the brilliance of their decision to purchase such a long-lasting and worthwhile brand and how we would never sell subpar quality. Reinforcing each ego-driven nugget of opportunity keeps the sale moving in a positive direction. Slowly we prodded the customer to feel more comfortable making the significant purchase decision. You must qualify your brand as "worthwhile" in the customer's mind. I encouraged customers to close, using as much expertise from my experience, by ensuring they couldn't imagine purchasing this from anyone else. I needed to leave them with a confirmation that they were making the best decision. See how that works? Even if the customer is still determining if they are ready to purchase, it's my job to work their ego and keep them moving in that positive closing direction.

Essentially with brand qualifying, you need to build **exclusivity or uniqueness** around your brand. Proving the quality of our services or products to the client naturally increases our chances of closing sales. As sales representatives, we should ensure clients seek to find their self-esteem within our brand. Remember, we must target the ego of the customer.

A successful brand using **exclusivity** is Cambria Surfaces. Over the years, I've watched this brand grow and include and exclude the customer base. For years they have implemented a strategy of "We are the Lexus of countertops." They created a VIP feel for their trade show events, locking out the average consumer and creating a feeling of elegance. Another brand exemplifying expertise is Antolini-Italy. This company uses an appearance of luxury and exclusivity, and over sixty-plus years built a loyal following. They exhibit a tendency to disassociate themselves from the general public at trade events. The concept of exclusion propels customers to desire more information. The act of maintaining secrecy motivates certain customers to aspire to be part of the source of the mystique. What about brands within your industry? Keep in mind exclusivity doesn't always correlate to expensive either.

It could be a **unique** feature instead, giving the impression only your product has this. Manolo Blahnik shoes has a reputation for having red bottoms. Red bottom shoes are mentioned in R&B, Pop, and Hip Hop songs across American culture, creating association and **exclusivity** in a specific demographic. How about the Brioni suit or the Bulova watch you might have seen in a *Swagger* magazine at the barber shop? Showcasing people who look like those in the barbershop using these brands pairs the target market with exclusivity and helps the client identify with it. If the brand is more luxurious than a consumer can afford or is sold in a retailer not close by, seeing it in the barbershop creates an illusion of reachability. Something those in the shop can strive to achieve. This hits that ego nugget of wanting to belong. A perfect example of targeted marketing in a specific retail environment.

Organized team effort

Capturing leads is a team effort! Leads might originate from marketing, advertising, brand presence, or post-sale foundations! We most certainly collect leads as salespeople.

As we discussed in the first section, identifying missing **organizational** skills will optimize our ability to do our jobs. One important role for any salesperson is assisting with lead management. If you've started incorporating organizational strategy into your daily routine, you're on your way to adopting new lead capture and qualification techniques. Starting with an **organized plan** is crucial in sales. If the company you work for has a CRM, great! Are you using the CRM's data reporting to its fullest intent? Do you enter data daily: record visits, attach accounts, and create referrals? Are you using a CRM to process project timelines? I recommend that all companies consider upgrading to start implementing a CRM into their teams day-to-day immediately. These systems process sales data and manage our account data far better than humans can process the same data in a spreadsheet. While this book isn't about CRM systems, I do want you to learn how to better capture and qualify leads to move into the sales process, which is when we actually close sales.

Follow-Up

Follow-up is as much a key component in lead nurture as it is in the sales process. Later in the book I go into detail about all the "right times" to follow up and suggest some methods you probably haven't thought of for finding old leads that require some nurturing. Before we move on, I want to impart the importance once again of this little adjunct verb in not only collecting and nurturing leads but eventually closing sales. Referring back to my initial story, follow-up and consistency

53

during the lead process are what makes sales reps "order makers, not order takers". We have to follow up on leads if they are ever going to become sales prospects. We cannot wait for clients to walk in our doors or visit our website, we have to nurture them into signing contracts. We do that by staying on top of potential leads and nurturing them into the sales process.

Section 3

Sales Process—On Your Mark, Get Ready, Sell

Welcome to the heart of this book: the actual art of selling. I want you to take detailed notes as we discuss the sales process flow.

Chapter 6
PRACTICE YOUR PITCH

Starting us off in the selling process is the sales pitch. Improving yours is as simple as following the acronym, PITCH.

Problem solver

Before walking into a meeting or appointment, be ready to listen to the client's problems and be the solution they require. This element of listening and coming to the rescue will help you win the close, especially if you're selling services.

Inspire to action

Every pitch and every close requires you to have questions ready to fire so you can gain as much information as possible from each client and push them toward booking with you! You must take the customer to the next step without them realizing it! Have you heard the term ABC, always be closing?

This old-fashioned sales phrase means inspiring action and utilizing questions to move your client toward closing the deal. So call your client out and into action! Examples of questions that inspire action:

- Will you be ready by Tuesday?

- Can we start the program on July 1st?

- Is Wednesday next week available so we can schedule a delivery?

- Will someone be home next Tuesday so we can lock in your service appointment?

Tailor your style

My favorite pitch technique, this one, requires intelligent guessing and using those **chameleoning** skills. Scientists have captured the attunement of emotions in the laboratory by measuring the physiology—such as heart rate—of two people sharing a good conversation. As the interaction begins, their bodies operate at different rhythms. But after 15 minutes, the physiological profiles of their bodies look remarkably similar."[3] A phenomenon called "mirroring." While tailoring our styles might come close to crossing a line of "being fake," our goal is to align our personalities with the client. We are on the offensive, attempting to win the sale, and on the defensive, listening for clues about the deal's likelihood

---

3   Daniel Goleman et al., "Primal Leadership: The Hidden Driver of Great Performance," Harvard Business Review, December 2001, https://hbr. org/2001/12/primal-leadership-the-hidden-driver-of-great-performance.

of closing. We must switch gears at any time to keep the client and conversation in the right direction. Changing our style to fit those we are working with helps keep us coloring between the lines. If I work with a soft-spoken librarian type, I'll lower my voice and hold back on the vulgar comments. If I work with someone loud and gregarious, I can be more like my usual self. You get the picture.

Be concise

Keep your pitches concise. Be straightforward and keep it moving. As that inner nurturing system develops, a salesperson learns when they are tiring out the other party verbally. Learning to use fewer words to accomplish the same task is an art form. The less time wasted, the better. If you (or the client) move too far from the sale conversation, you might miss the sale altogether. Have you ever been in a meeting where just before you got to the point, someone's phone rang and the decision-maker had to leave the room? Don't waste time. Get to the point; there will be time for socializing and chatting after you close the deal.

Heart

Do you love what you do? Do you have any passion for what you're selling? We are better salespeople when we find faith in our products and services. We must believe in what we are selling to convince anyone to purchase from us.

Rep Methods used the following pitch to build a book launch team. We used everything mentioned above to work for this action-oriented sales pitch, and we got results right away! Within seventy-two hours we had ten people to add to our launch team.

> Hey XXX! I noticed you've clicked on all my stuff lately. Thank you!

> Will you commit to being a part of my book launch team? I have three options for you to choose from.

> Please don't just read this. I need you to respond with the one option which works for you. It doesn't hurt my feelings how you participate; I simply want you to be a part of this.

> There are only a few select people on this specialty ask, and I really want to thank you for all your support today and going forward. I drafted a video to tell you all about this special event; take a peek.

> Option 1: Buy a discounted copy and post a review ASAP! Then, share with a few people you know. (EARLY RELEASE)

> Option 2: Buy a discounted copy and review it on Amazon immediately! (EARLY RELEASE)

> Option 3: Buy the book on Launch Day!

Notice how we created a solution to our problem by creating an ask right out the gate? No reason to dilly around anyone's attention span. In this particular sales pitch, I'm not solving a customer's problem, I am the one with the ask, but I was concise and jumped right into the problem I needed solved. I showed my heart in the video (which is now posted on our YouTube channel, if you want to check it out). This creates a tailored style, meeting the audience's preference for video, and the visual elements drive home the task and show passion for the project at the same time. The entire pitch is prompting action, with definitive questions and a request for a decision and a response. Then, in the end, we pitch to our clients' egos by letting them know they are part of a select group. We engage and control the sales by providing three options—not participating or "opting out" isn't one of the three options.

Just like with those lead and sale qualifying questions, our pitch and how we listen, react, and devise or customize our approach toward each client can be the make-or-break difference in whether we will close a sale today. We must use all the information we gained during the lead process to apply a "pitch" perfect for each client successfully.

Chapter 7

MERCHANDISING SALES

This magical little topic of merchandising sales is huge. It gives me a unique advantage point compared to other sales trainers. Through proper merchandising, I built better relationships as a product representative, increased my overall sales numbers, provided clients with a complete package, and earned a larger sale for the store. As I'm working with younger salespeople, I often get twisted looks of confusion when I bring up merchandising as a selling technique. Merchandising isn't just for those of us peeking in the windows on 5th Avenue. "Merchandising is everything you do to promote and sell your products once the potential customer is in your store."[4] Merchandising is about the presentation of products or services. As a sales rep, it's not always inside the store, as this quote suggests; sometimes we bring the merchandising directly to the customer. Merchandising as a sales tactic builds customer loyalty while controlling the attention

---

4   "What Is Merchandising? Definition and Guide," Shopify (blog), November 11, 2022, https://www.shopify.com/blog/what-is-merchandising.

of our clients. Typically, we are talking about products and manufacturers regarding merchandising, but any brand can be merchandised, even if it's a service.

While studying marketing at the university, we first learned about branding using Kleenex as a keen example. Do you buy tissues or purchase Kleenex? Do you ask for ibuprofen or Advil? Those with brand loyalty will buy the name-brand items. Take the SPANX brand, for instance: this billion-dollar, 100 percent privately owned brand sells its product in major department store retailers and within SPANX's retail locations nationwide. What about the SPANX brand keeps customers returning to its products and brand year after year? With humble beginnings in lingerie, the brand has expanded into ready-to-wear apparel. The creator of SPANX, Sara Blakely, began her merchandising strategy with a small hanging rack in the back of the hosiery section at Nordstrom, but over time, she observed most of her clients checked out in the suits department. During the crucial moments of her trial sales period within this department store, she shifted her strategy and moved the display to a flat counter space at the checkout area in the women's suit department. She did this without permission; however, breaking the rules paid off as sales started to pour in once the retail associates became comfortable showing the product to the customers trying on suits. Sara used a brand strategy of observation and the sales process strategy of merchandising to make the product easy for a client to pick up during a purchase. Proper merchandising can propel a brand into a household name. Women don't go to department stores now and ask for "undergarments." Instead, they walk in the doors and ask for SPANX.

As my skill in merchandising became increasingly important to my client's success within the wholesale industry, I became their first call. So how do we stand out? How do we set ourselves apart? How do you merchandise a service? How can you merchandise your brand to fit in amongst the competition? And finally, how does this correlate to increasing your sales and overall profits?

There are five adjectives to consider when identifying merchandising: **placement, style, cleanliness, convenience,** and **ease.**

Placement

With products, placement is the most apparent merchandising tactic. If we're thinking about shelf space, the psychology behind a shelf's placement has to do with the consumer's eye level. For example, lower prices and off-priced brands are typically on the lower shelves in the grocery store. For showrooms, you want to place the most expensive and exclusive (better markup or margin) items in front of the showroom, closest to the presentation/meeting area. This way, when working with a client, the products that produce the most revenue are the easiest to grab during a consultation.

In regards to services, place your brand where it's convenient for customers to use you. Sometimes this is obvious, such as hair supplies in a salon, but my challenge for today's reader is to look beyond the low-hanging fruit. Try connecting with co-op businesses that can make your service shine. Often, I see business cards laid neatly up at a reception desk in an attempt to co-op business-to-business merchandising. But simply placing your business card or flyer on the counter won't do much. Instead, you need to coordinate with the person working the front desk, or other in-house personnel who would be responsible for referring to your merchandised service, to refer you. If you are a service provider and utilize other companies to display your company, make sure you're educating the personnel on how to help sell your service. Don't forget to thank those referrals as well. It's just as important to follow up with thanks after receiving leads from co-op service marketing.

Style

When considering merchandising **style**, consider a brand's overall appearance. Do the logo colors correspond with the colors in the retail showroom? Does your brand package fit the same style as the vehicles your team drives? Does your "look" blend in with the brand?

Sometimes, we don't have a say in a brand's appearance. For example, you might get stuck selling a brand priced like a brand-new Lexus that looks like a Kia Soul from 2006. How do you get around these selling barriers? You may have to get creative! One technique I have used is to forget the entire collection and focus on the winning item or items that have a better chance of success. For example, when selling a collection of surfaces with 120 colors, many outdated and not on trend, I opt to pare down any display to six or eight winning colors. I have to change the customer's focus away from the ugly and worn-out selections which can weigh down a brand's overall appearance. I'm helping my client and their customer look past the price point and focus on the successful elements of the brand.

Keep it clean!

It's problematic that, as managers and owners, we must constantly remind our staff of the importance of reracking samples and cleaning the windowsills. What about keeping the presentation area of a vehicle vacuumed and organized? Have you ever had to ride with a sales representative who needed to vacuum the food from the baby car seats and your passenger seat? Imagine what a customer sees when that vehicle shows up on their property.

Merchandising keeps the presentation clean, influencing the egos of our customers. It's an easy, cost-effective, and time-conscience step to ensuring no barriers to sale. This is the same for services as well! Find new ways of presenting your service and brand within those co-op environments that help you stand out and keep it maintained. Perhaps, you need to set a schedule to follow up with those co-op service companies to see what needs to be done to refresh and tidy up your service's presentation.

Be convenient

You need to **merchandise your clients as well as your products**. Identify new business clients best suited to your brand, size, and aesthetic. For example, in the commercial specification world, we talk about leads in terms of low-hanging fruit versus more complicated projects. When I'm searching for the right target audience to get my product on specification, I want to make sure my product or service is convenient in its selection to the architect or designer. This might require multiple library visits to ensure the materials are updated. This might require multiple continuing education presentations to be sure the teams involved consider me the expert in this field and increase my chances of becoming the first call. I must ensure my product is easy, convenient, and on the specifiers' minds. In established territories, many merchandised service relationships exist already. It's my job to penetrate and showcase how my product or service can improve, replace, or complement existing relationships. Showcasing complementary tactics encourages a smoother transition if I come in as a new product or service. Start by examining the best business relationships already in place. A properly merchandised product or service brand leaves no stone unturned (pardon the industry pun) in its search for new business. As we mentioned in style, some companies might require smaller displays for products, so get creative and make it convenient.

Be easy

A well-merchandised product or service becomes the easy button. And the salesperson just needs to be reliable, answer the phone, respond well with a follow-up, and be an expert in their field. Referring to the expertise chapter, an expert merchandising salesperson ensures customers remain informed about product and service advantages. It's imperative to remember that salespeople sell what they understand, what they like, and what's easy. This might require you to spend extra time with co-op company representatives to ensure they're properly trained for your service or product.

If you're selling a product, schedule monthly product knowledge reviews and maintain displays, keeping the overall appearance of the brand clean, new, and fresh. You must expedite instructions and information regarding all changes in a product quickly and efficiently. Service merchandising requires consistently updating clients on changes in fees, packages, and/or new recommendations you want to be discussed with a potential client.

How to master a sale with merchandising in five

If you sell products and visit clients to discuss replenishment orders, implement these steps into every visit—starting today.

Step one—Know your inventory: This technique works from fashion to flooring. If stock constantly changes, figure out a method to keep up. We must take the time out of our week to study, memorize, and know our inventory.

Step two—Count your inventory: Upon arrival at the client's location and before you speak to them, count and take a quick inventory upon arrival. What has sold and what's still on the floor, yard, shelf, etc.? Record the counts and make notes in your CRM, device notes, planner, etc.

Step three—Take notes: Meet with the client briefly and present what has sold since your last visit and what you currently have in stock that would complement what they already have. Start the conversation by congratulating them on a successful month. Next, ask for advice and information regarding product performance. Make sure to take notes. Would they like to see similar options? You will know what to suggest based on sales history if you know your inventory. Are there multiple sales associates? Should you be talking to each of them?

Listen to your client and let them tell you what to sell them!

Step four—Send offers: Use those notes when you are back in the warehouse or home office to make a new product offer to the client. You have easy sales at your fingertips if your sole job is refilling sold materials they use regularly. Your knowledge of incoming inventory will become helpful when making suggestions of alternatives if an item is not available.

Use the latest inventory information, photos, and price deals where possible.

Step five—Follow up: We must follow up in various sequences. After twenty-four hours start with a text or a phone call to ensure the client receives your message and pushes the sale. Within forty-eight hours, follow up to see if they have decided. If they need more time, ask them when you should check back to close the deal. For those of us who schedule regular visits, we can use that offer on the next visit and push the client to make the decision in person. Use the data you already have to help you close! Stay humble! If you miss the sale for any reason, ask questions. You will build confidence with information for the next opportunity and may guilt your buyer into buying something from you on the next occasion. I guarantee the success of this process and welcome feedback from all who implement this into their daily routine.

This five-step method is a perfect segue for discussing controlling the sale. At Rep Methods controlling the sale is how ***"We make order makers, not order takers."*** This five-step merchandising method allows our "accounts," our clients, to become dependent on our skills in managing their inventory. You might even become an exclusive salesperson because you've spoiled them with your new techniques. Call up a few of my former clients in Virginia and ask them yourself! I guarantee that a few of my former customers (not all) became dependent on my merchandising and controlling sale methods to fulfill their inventory needs. As master salespersons, we should tailor sales pitches to each client and change the delivery angles to fit each scenario. My success working for a wholesale distributor as a slab, bundle, and container saleswoman was built on these simple tactics and day-to-day merchandising techniques. Please write to me and tell me how well this new strategy has worked to change the dynamic of your sales. Info@repmethods.com.

Chapter 8

CONTROLLING SALES

Mastering your technique for selling and improving your closing rate depends on your ability to stylishly control the sale as it happens. Lead your client where you want them to go. Take the initiative to remain humble and listen and guide the customer into the closing process. Let's look at some of these strategies.

Listening

Listening is an essential controlling sales tactic and is a craft you need to develop. Unfortunately, type A personalities often overlook it. I've seen a few outgoing professionals fail at the art of selling because they need to shut up more to let the consumer lead them to the close. We will discuss this more in the closing of the sale section, but listening is imperative in learning that gut instinct and when to shift conversations and move into sales pitching. We must **listen** to gain cues from our customers. Listen and use your eyes to notice if we are losing the audience, or if they are moving away from a win. Sometimes the customer will walk you right into the sale by asking the right questions and using the "pre-selling" preparation.

Knowing when to hold and when to fold

This poker-playing innuendo is a fun way of referring to finding your intuition when your price is getting too low. If they're asking for too low a price, it is time to *fold*. We must always *hold* the integrity of a product and its margins. Far too many times, I have witnessed a competitor winning a deal using a price I could never match. Is a sale worth winning if the company loses money? Unfortunately, this is the case in specific bottom-feeding, bulk-selling organizations. It's better to find a customer willing to pay your price than to move goods at a loss.

So hold your ground and don't go too low. Developing the gut instinct to wait, to hold, to pull back from pressure is a key component of the art of selling. In this book I've outlined some of the psychology behind customers' decision making. We then need to use our "limbic resonance" and ability to feel out when the customer we are pitching to isn't quite ready to close this deal. From there, we learn to back off, to bend, to curve, to hold for a future sale. We learn to take notes on what almost closed but didn't quite make the cut. We adapt, returning to the client with our updated knowledge prepared to repeat the pitch, tailoring its verbiage toward our new understanding of what the client needs to close the deal. This, my friends, is knowing when to hold and when to fold.

Limiting the options

You need to begin to limit the options you present to a client. For example, I'll use flooring finishing as an option in direct selling. If you are a flooring salesperson with 120 colors to select, do you walk into the home with 120 possibilities? Yes, however, you only present a few of those options simultaneously. Start with three at a time.

I teach reps to work in teams of three. I am no psychologist and have zero data to back up what is happening in the brain's frontal cortex for the number three, but I promise you that the magic number is three. We might review several styles and items needing decisions, but we don't present the options at once. Factories often produce a sampling of goods in options A, B, or C. Clients will make quicker decisions by limiting their selections.

To narrow the choices, some designers I have worked for in the past direct clients to their YouTube channels before meeting in person to help narrow down the customizations by letting the customer decide in advance. Could you use photos of finished projects to narrow down the options before you have to carry 120 colors from your car?

*Pro tip—Limiting your options in advance works as a **pre-selling technique**.

If you use a merchandising strategy and help identify weaknesses in your customer's stocking inventory, you're also controlling the sale. You're using that humble initiative to work for your client and provide them with easy solutions by using you and your products now and in the future. You have become reliable. If you listen properly to what the customers need and why they came into your store today, you can walk them right toward the product and educate them on why they chose you, your brand, and your company to make the right decision for their needs today. All clients are simply looking for you to solve their problems. And you do that while controlling the sale and easing the mind of that consumer with your valuable expertise. When you qualify your brands or services to meet the needs of the customer, you control the sale and directly increase the potential for a closing opportunity.

Chapter 9

CLOSING THE SALE

Closing is the most critical step in the sales process. Making money depends on our ability to win the deal. Previous chapters explained how the mind, ego, and brand are essential in selling to clients. As we've discovered, selling is a lot like a chess match. We must consider the moves of the opponent to corner them into a checkmate situation. Finally, we've qualified our company, product, or service.

Moving the sale from pitch to close is an integral part of actually closing sales. Over the years I've watched others continue to pitch and talk, never pushing or prodding the conversation to finish the deal. I've been guilty of this too. Keep in mind when you're crafting those pitch techniques, you want to **inspire your customers into action**, clinching the sale. To get that rolling, you must activate a conversation. If the client doesn't seem to be moving toward sealing the deal, keep returning to new action propositions, listen for actionable items, and move the conversation toward the transaction. For example, let's say you're in retail selling cell phones, and you've been reviewing the assets of the telephone and the packaged plan available in the client's budget and have pre-qualified your product for the customer, well, now it's time to get them to the checkout. That's when you push the client to transfer the phone line, discuss payment plans, and what credit card they want to keep on file.

During the sales pitch I want you to include those inspiring action questions and listen for the answers, then assume the order, write the order, and make them stop you. When you begin to hear the answers you need to complete the sale, it's time to start writing up that contract and moving the client into the final stages to close.

Have you ever watched sales training videos from older corporate strategies? If so, you may have heard, "Assume the order, write the order, and make them stop you." This simple shift in attitude can change your sales closing percentages. Making them stop you is an aggressive technique I urge salespeople to use gingerly. We want to pull them to the table to finish and sign the final paperwork, not force customers into sales they aren't requesting. Make sure you understand the difference. Use action questions or, even better, action statements that draw that sale to a close! Insert action questions like "Can I deliver the X I sent you in last week's offer that you asked me to hold?" Or make assertive statements the customer will need to correct or reverse, such as "No problem. We will deliver Thursday." In my experience listening to salespeople, some ask far too many questions and make fewer statements giving away that control. Be assertive.

Let's visit some examples.

Ask what telephone line they're moving over to X and let them know you need to begin that process. Ask which credit card they want to use for the new phone and if they would like to go ahead and put one on file for monthly payments. Typically, many phone companies offer a discount if you sign up for autopay, so now is an excellent opportunity to remind them of the savings each month when they put that credit card on file. If they hesitate, remind them how easy it is to update the credit card online and change this information anytime. Finally, move into this process seamlessly and close out the sale. Voila!

If you work in retail apparel and the client has spent an hour trying on suits in the dressing room, it's time to narrow their purchase selections. Don't simply ask to remove their unwanted items; instead, ask, "Which ones are we keeping"? Be sure to state, "I'm going to take these out of your way and hang them up front." This **"controlling the sale"** technique will increase the likelihood of the client sending you to the front with items they wish to purchase. Women often categorize clothing items as either desirable or not while in the dressing room. You're **providing a solution** to the client and one that works toward a sale, not a cleaning position. At this moment, closing the sale becomes imperative, and shifting gears to increasing the numeric value will come shortly after you identify what items you have to accessorize the winning selections.

If you're selling windows and visiting a cold-call lead, it's safe to assume that, at some point, the client will purchase windows. You must secure their purchase with your company rather than the other company. So go through the steps I have outlined:

- Go through your tailored sales pitch with confidence.

- Make sure you listen after including facts on expertise and qualifying that brand.

- Proceed to write up the sales sheet or fill out the iPad criteria regardless of how it's going.

- Ask the customer for bits and pieces of the forms' data requests as you move along the sales pitch. "Can I get the planned install date you are thinking of?" "I want to double-check that this package fits your budget." "What is the monthly payment that you're considering?"

Take a few minutes and write out some action questions and assertive statements to better prepare for your next sales engagement. Then, let's talk about how you will also need to battle the inevitable client refusal during this process.

Chapter 10
REBUTTALS AND REFUSALS

The **rebuttal and refusal** process during a sale is often the most challenging technique to develop for any B2B or B2C salesperson. How are we supposed to change their minds? How are we supposed to bring a win when it's heading for a loss? If you're in direct sales, this can be the most challenging skill to master. In my experience, we can't win every deal. I once had a manager who reminded me of that as I occasionally stormed around the office in defeat. It wasn't pretty. Most salespeople don't like to lose. However, many of us will do anything for the win. The rebuttal and refusal processes are like a chess match; the best **listener** wins! That's right, listening is coming up once again as a technique. **Listening** and reading body language are the first clues to mastering this ping-pong match. Another key is knowing your brand's value, which we have already discussed. Then add to that specific rebuttal and refusal techniques I've learned over the years, and you can handle this difficult step:

- knowing your role
- knowing the competition
- understanding the customer
- re-prompting a sale
- bluffing back into a deal
- knowing when to walk away

Knowing your role

What do you mean, Alison? I'm the salesperson, duh! Are you the salesperson, or are you a messenger? Are you there to make the sale, or are you there to create a future opportunity? See yourself more as a messenger, offering a great opportunity.

Once you see yourself as a messenger, you can use that knowledge in the rebuttal. Softly speak your message. I say softly spoken because we want to use this technique and verbiage mildly yet firmly reminding the client of our message.

Let's say you're selling windows, and while giving your sales pitch, you notice the customer squirming and losing eye contact, so you feel you're losing the sale. In my experience, I feel in my gut that I'm losing them. At that point, we must make a shift in the conversation. You're not a salesperson; you're a messenger. So stop pitching and start asking questions. Then use their answers to guide how you will state the message. How you will inform, create exclusivity, and deliver the message that the client would be crazy purchasing from anyone else. For example,

"Mrs. Jones, I can see you might be tired of hearing about XXXX attributes, so shall we move into color selections, or have I missed any key information you were looking to learn? I want to make sure you've heard all the information that made you reach out to us initially, and by no means am I here to waste your time."

Softly spoken, this method of knowing my role shows the customer I'm serious about making them happy and providing all the knowledge *they* need to make an informed decision. By reading their body language and essentially calling them out on what looked like a loss of interest, I let the customer guide me into the next steps of our conversation. It's amazing to watch their reaction, as I'm recognizing and re-affirming my role as the informer, the expert, the guide to their selections.

Knowing your competition

If I'm selling windows and visiting the client's home, then nine times out of ten, the customer wants me there. But likely I'm not the first salesperson to have visited Mrs. Jones. If Mrs. Jones wants a new house full of windows, she's done some research and has come prepared with data, so I should too. I need to know who the direct competitors are, be equipped with the pros and cons, and be ready to fire off the brand's advantages at any moment. Remember **"owning the brand"**? Remember all those qualifications: we must separate our brand from the competition. Often during the rebuttal process, this information becomes the most helpful. Prepare to use this knowledge to win back the client's faith and confidence in what you are selling.

Understanding the customer

Understanding the customer will assist in the ongoing boxing match that is sales. It's an inevitable "bobbing and weaving" some days around refusals. If I have a history of visiting a client who notoriously wastes my time by engaging in product review then blows me off at the end due to lack of funds, it's my job to ensure the next time I make a sales call with this client I pre-qualify the opportunity with a question: "How are you today, Mr. Jung? What's your slab budget available this week? Shall we review photos of bundles in the budget?"

Now when I walk into the sale, I've removed the opportunity for this client to back away over budget. If the client engages in reviewing the product, they won't be able to escape because I've pre-qualified the purchase possibilities in advance.

Sometimes it's our job to be a therapist. Sometimes it's our job to get an attitude and walk out because the customer is an a-hole; they don't deserve our attention. Well, that last one is an example of a tough day. We've all been there.

Re-prompting a customer into a sale

I encourage all salespeople to learn how to **re-prompt a customer into a sale**. I prefer re-prompting and creating action questions over the bluffing and walking away tactics. Sales engagement doesn't have to be a boxing match; it should be a fun game of cat and mouse. A fun game leaves everyone feeling happy; whereas if you get into a boxing match, it can cause issues. I refer to my favorite quote from the character played by Tom Hanks in *A League of Their Own*: "There's no crying in baseball." If we're about to lose a sale, why not push a few questions or assertive statements to reengage the client and bring them back into the deal?

Try reminding the client what brought you to them initially. Most likely they had a problem needing a solution, and you still have that solution. Did you **listen** and gather any facts about that problem? Are they on a specific time limit that only you can remedy? Are there parameters in choosing your company over the competition? Do you need to remind them of some of the brand qualifications? It's our job to shift the movement from negativity and denial back into positive remedies. Bring up or ask questions about deadlines. Can you change the perspective back to completing the purchase today? Do you need to ask the customer directly what the holdup or perceived issue is preventing them from closing right now? Sometimes a direct approach allows a salesperson to solve their problem again, reminding them relief is in sight.

Bluffing and walking away

Most of my tactic strategies come with war stories. In my career selling stone, bluffing and walking away get used daily.

The market has top competition, so challenging negotiation skills are required. My industry comes with diverse clients from international backgrounds and cultures. The granite business in specific areas has been a "race to the bottom" for many years.

When it comes to the rebuttal and refusal process, salespeople must know everything they can about the pricing flexibility, cost of goods, and markup, if possible in order to reengage. Yet many owners and company management prefer to keep this information private, so that's when **bluffing** may need to come into play. For example, I remember a **$15,000** sale negotiated to an uncomfortable margin threshold for one of my regular customers. This gentleman got me to agree to a lower price than I wanted, but I needed the sale, so I decided to make the deal. When the truck arrived at his facility, he called me to complain about a crack in the material on one corner. He wanted a more significant discount. Unfortunately, my chameleon skills came into play on that phone call. I say unfortunately because mimicking him meant screaming because he often raises his voice to push me into doing what he wants. A screaming match ensued, which left some of my coworkers staring at me in disbelief. I politely (not really) told the gentleman where he could go, and if he didn't like the material, to put it back on the truck and send it back. I told him I wasn't interested in his business if he sent back perfectly good material at an already amazing price. I let him know the price was already lower than the market rate and below our margin thresholds. It was a superb deal and the material defect in one small corner didn't warrant a further discount. I made it clear if he sent it back, we were done and would never conduct business with him. The bluff worked; I won. He kept the material, and I made the sale. I'm not proud of the arguing, but I had to match his heat. I hope as a salesperson, you can understand that sometimes there is a necessity to rebut a heated tone by matching it, and I refused his masochistic approach by not letting him beat me down in price. The company made a profit, and we all moved on. The key to bluffing is knowing the mindset of your customer. **Preparing to walk away and lose a sale is sometimes the most effective way to win.** (Although it's not always pretty.)

A quick note: As we have discussed, rejection, losses, and some more hostile and challenging experiences in sales and business development are a part of the process. We can only win some engagement. So keep your heads up, friend! Find a channel for some of the negativity. Find time in positive practices to keep moving forward; keep practicing that expertise. Positive coping mechanisms will foster a happy and healthy career.

Chapter 11
FOLLOW UP—PLEASE

Follow-up is by far the most valuable and underused skill in a salesperson's toolkit. Following up with customers is the key to building fruitful, reliable sales and relationships! Unfortunately, follow-up takes practice, and it can feel uncomfortable. Most salespeople need to learn this essential skill, yet many prefer avoiding difficult things. As an example, read the conversation between myself and a budding salesperson during a morning meeting (I ask about follow-up during every Monday morning meeting). The conversations usually went like this:

> **Salesperson:** "I visited the such-and-such company and reviewed their inventory. I noticed they are running low on Valle Nevado, so I told Miguel we have bundles for seven ninety-five."
>
> **Trainer:** "Fantastic. Did he buy the bundle?"
>
> **Salesperson:** "No, he wanted to wait until Friday."

89

Trainer: "Awesome. Did you follow up?"

Salesperson: "Not yet."

Trainer: "Why not yet?"

Salesperson: "Because we got so busy on Friday."

Trainer: "You forgot?"

Salesperson: "Yes, I'll do it today."

Trainer: "Wonderful; why don't you put a note on your calendar next time so you don't forget to follow up?"

Salesperson: "Sure. Good idea."Later that morning...

Trainer: "Did you call Miguel?"

Salesperson: "Yes, he bought the bundle from XXX competitor."

Trainer: "Ugh, sounds like you missed the sale."

Salesperson: "Yes, I'll get it next time."

This salesperson will only get them next time if they learn to follow up. If we don't take the time to follow up with our clients, we miss sales.

Perhaps you work retail and think there is no follow-up in retail, as you rely on clients entering the store. Are you a salesperson waiting for Godot to arrive? A personal shopper doesn't wait for the person to walk in the door. A refined personal shopper scurries when fresh inventory arrives, as they telephone their favorite and loyal clients to alert them of the new product's arrival.

This scenario goes for all salespeople. If we are proactive in selling and alerting clients about new arrivals, we create sales opportunities. We put in tremendous effort, making their mouths salivate in becoming the first company to pounce on this new arrival or inventory. What is the purpose of taking notes, counting inventory, and flashing new products if we spend less time following up with clients? **Follow-up** is the make-or-break scenario between an order maker and an order taker. Order making prompt sales, while following up closes deals.

General follow-up

Follow-up fosters a strong sense of urgency, increasing the likelihood of closing a sale. Follow-up is an essential motivating factor in any successful sales strategy.

It can be performed before the sale, during the sale, or after the sale. Surprised? It sounds like an after-action, right? But follow-up can also prepare a client for a visitor to create an opportunity for later interaction. So use follow-up as a scheduling tool.

Following up **before** a sale means preparing the client for a new meeting, phone call, visit, appointment, etc., by letting them know what you intend to show and what you've discussed previously. A recap follow-up prior to a sales attempt prepares the client to make a decision. Sometimes our customers need to be reminded of our meeting and business focus. So to make the process smoother and waste less of everyone's time, outline your intentions for the meeting in a follow-up.

Following up **during** a sale? Yes! Especially if you are using a computer or other technology to show a product. Make sure to have the previously communicated product opportunities loaded and ready to show. For example, when I sell slabs, I visit customers' inventory facilities and try to tempt them into buying new products. Before I go into the appointment, I make sure to pull up the last few material offers so I can remind the customer *during the sale* of opportunities I've made for them previously. This is a great way to seal a deal on the spot! People forget, they are busy, they have business to attend to, so we are there to remind them of the opportunities available during a sales pitch.

A key to following up is ensuring that all communication methods and "touches" are investigated for missed opportunities. It's an **"easy button"** in finding sales.

Here lies the conundrum. Most failures in post-sale follow-up happen because the responsibility hasn't been assigned nor communicated! However, if you, the salesperson, your boss, or whoever discusses when and how the company will implement the follow-up, you can have clear directions and steps to ensure it's happening. So here are the steps to carry out your team's to-do list today.

Follow up with email

Doesn't everything happen through emails? You're filing your emails away each week, as discussed in the organization chapter, right? Remember my story from my early days in New York where the VP of sourcing stopped by my desk each week to check if I'd emptied my inbox? From that I developed the habit of reading my email history, and follow-up became second nature.

You must check your sent emails. I provide this little nugget in my online classes as a *100 percent guarantee*. This little trick is *guaranteed* to change your sales and follow-up game. Each week, set aside about an hour to review the sent mail from the previous week. If you do this once a month, you are guaranteed to find a lost sales opportunity. I typically save these moments for a Friday afternoon when I'm tired of driving and interacting with customers face-to-face.

Within the surfaces industry, many of our customers start work very early, and by five p.m. on a Friday, they are checked out for the week. Therefore, Friday nights are an excellent time to prepare follow-ups for the next week. In addition, I send responses to unanswered emails and make notes on my calendar to fix gaps in the schedule for next week. Finally, it helps to set that to-do list for Monday so I can enjoy the weekend.

When I send my follow-up on Friday nights, my customers will catch them first thing Monday morning, making me the first call of the week.

Follow up with social media

Does your company promote new products on social channels? How is the response? Do you follow the channels? Are you the channel manager? Social media is another opportunity for follow-up. Depending on how actively your company interacts with the public, look for opportunities to make new relationships or create new sales opportunities. This follow-up method can help turn a cold call into a warm call or create opportunities for questions leading to a sales push.

Follow up with texting

In 2023, texting has taken over the norms of communication. Have you ever scrolled through your work phone text history looking for sales leads? Magically, a conversation will appear that was once forgotten—a reply overlooked. You may have been driving and forgotten to reply.

Follow up in person

The "text" or the "email" follow-up has become a safety net and doesn't always win sales. I believe in the importance of human interaction, so let me warn all my readers that if you follow up via text or email, you may be setting yourself up to lose a sale. The impersonal method of texting or emailing someone also allows them to respond with a "no thanks" if they respond at all. Remember, follow-up initiated using impersonal communication warrants impersonal replies. In my experience, success comes more often using a personal approach. I urge readers to weigh options carefully with following up on a sale. This means making the phone call! Making the in-person appointment. Spending time to re-enforce your offers and increasing success by putting follow-up on the table one on one. You will close more sales.

As you can see, **follow-up** is imperative to the success of an inside or outside salesperson. Timing can and should vary. Learning to feel out of the moment takes practice. Sometimes our gut instinct tells us, "It's too soon," "I should wait," or "I don't want to pressure *X*." I have said these very phrases on multiple occasions. Oddly enough, the development of comfortability in making someone reach for the phone to follow up is a transcending moment of growth in a salesperson's career. Find the courage to make the phone call.

Ahh, doesn't that feel better? You now know all the ways follow-up can and will improve your sales. So, if you do nothing else from this book, please learn to **follow up**.

Section 4

Post-Sale Foundations

An old biblical proverb mentions building a house on sand vs. building a house on a rock foundation. Whether this is a spiritual or physical house, this proverb remains true in literal translation. You wouldn't build your house on sand without installing proper concrete footers specified in the building code. Foundation matters. In business, the **post-sale foundation** is as important as the close. Setting the tone for future business must be a strategy, not an afterthought.

You may be thinking, "I'm a sales rep. What the hell do I have to do with post-sale foundations? That's somebody else's job." How are salespeople related to the post-sale foundation? If we want to **change**, **inspire**, and **support** a business through selling, we must recognize the recurrent importance of post-sale foundations. Our work as sales and business development people can make or break the future business of an organization. Post-sale customer relationship is crucial. We should secure their **satisfaction** with the product or service. By offering other **opportunities for engagement**, such as those surveys and review opportunities, we motivate our customers to keep coming back! Establishing a **repeat sale**, or a **word-of-mouth referral**, provides a larger payout than advertising alone. With the proper post-sale foundation methods, we, as salespeople, can set up a strong rapport with our customers and keep them returning time and time again.

Steps to strengthen your post-sales foundation

Step 1: Someone should send personalized emails (if possible) to customers thanking them for their purchase and letting them know you're available to answer any questions. The more personalized, the better. Not long ago, we did this with handwritten thank-you notes. While it's unnecessary to be this formal, consider the handwritten method if you close a large sale. Ask your boss if this could be added as an automation to the POS system or website.

Step 2: Ask the customer for feedback about their experience with your product or service. This feedback can help you improve your offerings and find testimonials for the website or marketing materials. We can learn from both positive and negative feedback and improve our expertise.

Another successful option to prompt future sales opportunities is to offer incentives for future purchases. As a wholesaler, I use this method every week. As I visit customers and follow up on their investments, I'm prompting the client with options to build more significant sales and create new sales. For example, I'll say, "Hey, Wes, if you pick up this bundle of Carrara, I'll send over these two soapstone slabs with a minor defect. You can use them, and I'd like to make the buy more valuable." Offering customers a discount or other incentive for their next purchase encourages repeat business and shows them that you value their loyalty.

Step 3: Use surveys and review requests. In 2023, businesses and authors rely heavily on reviews to promote future sales.

Hey, while we are talking about it, do you mind leaving me a raving review? If I didn't ask you to take a few moments out of your day to write a book review, I'd be losing a valuable opportunity. So go ahead and go online to where you bought this book and leave a review!

As you can see, integrating surveys and review requests into our sales process will allow you to create a foundation for future sales. If your company doesn't already have a system, I encourage implementing an after-sale survey and a link to leave a review. It's super easy to include this in an email signature or add it as an automation to your website.

As a salesperson, our direct impact on the outcome of a product or service review becomes a significant piece of the puzzle. When I teach sales processes for in-home selling agents, we discuss the "five stars" or "white glove" service angle.

These aren't my inventions. The concept of "steps of service" exists in many fields. Think about restaurants, food service, or the hospitality industry. We are creating a structure for how transactions "should" be executed. Creating ideal questions and responses for how salespeople and service personnel interact with the consumer makes a system for optimal results. As a salesperson, you can help establish and create those optimal outcomes for the entire sales process. Suggest to the owners or superiors how implementing an aftercare strategy into the sales process will help bring future business. Consider also how this will connect your business or product to other companies in the field. By implementing a proper foundation, we extend our network.

Step 4: Network. Another foundation often overlooked is the value of **networking** within our industry community. When I first started in the countertop business in 2011, the weight of implementing a brand strategy and building a failing reputation was on my shoulders. I wasn't "just" selling materials. How was I supposed to help develop the post-sale foundations? For me, it came through networking.

By **networking** with retailers and installers, I established co-op branding opportunities as part of the marketing strategy and strengthened our network.

In 2013, I challenged the local competitive brand to a pizza cook-off competition at a home show. The co-op marketing strategy served us both in several ways:

1. It showed the audience and our fellow remodeler communities that, as competitive brands, we could get along.
2. It allowed us both to present products on an equal playing field in a fun way and we both earned points in our networking groups.
3. It gave the consumer a window into the product world without shoving the brand down their throat.

We built foundations for future sales within the remodeling community and directly influenced consumers by showcasing the brand in a fun and competitive concept.

Volunteer

In 2018, I began volunteering for Women in Stone, a division of the Natural Stone Institute. In **volunteering**, I helped expose a secretive brand to a broader audience which played a role in the post-sale foundation. We built an annual event at the Stone Expo conference called "The Amazing Race." We modified an educational game from the television show. The game is a perfect example of a **marketing post-sale foundation** strategy because, as suppliers, we encouraged the participation of end-users such as designers, architects, retailers, and service groups (installers and fabricators). And these competitors competed in a fun and creative event that built brand promotion and informed them about products, creating recognition and a foundation for future sales.

You should start seeing results immediately by implementing these practices into your sales strategy.

Over the last decade, I have chosen various organization opportunities to volunteer, give back, and continue networking. I've been on boards and have served as president of chapters all the while learning and increasing my network. In 2023 I chose to volunteer, learn, and work with another fantastic give-back organization called NAWIC (National Association of Women in Construction www.nawic.

org). My local chapter #141 is already exceeding personal goals for continuing education. This year we will provide one week of construction education for twenty young females locally in seventh through ninth grades. Camp NAWIC (https://www.nawicrichmond.org/campnawic) encompasses over fifty local construction companies and organizations to provide exposure to the trade industry and help groom young females toward career opportunities in Construction. In 2022, NAWIC National provided approximately $180,000 in scholarships for students going into the trade. Through volunteering, networking, and a never-stop learning mentality, I enjoy my career, learn to give back, and keep thriving.

Final Words

MENTAL HEALTH AND SELLING

A last note. Mental health is a heavy topic in 2023. As a 1980s child, teen, or early adult, mental health was not discussed. However, our 2020–2023 society has been breaking down walls and discussing mental health more recently. I wanted to include this as a reality check for my fellow salespeople. Today's generations and future generations are prioritizing mental health and demanding employers take concerns and make resources accessible. It's personal to bring up mental health stresses and the struggle for balance working in sales roles, especially high-pressure or high-stress commissioned sales roles. I have worked for companies that promote alcohol as a highly accepted form of stress relief. But leaders should treat sales reps like corporate athletes instead of numbers on a dashboard. Sales representatives undergo significant levels of mental stress. So employers should expect employees to need time for psychological and physical rejuvenation.

Sales reps, just like athletes, need time to rejuvenate before and after the game. One way to do this is to take a sabbatical.

The New York Times just published an opinion piece by Tish Harrison Warren about taking sabbaticals. Tish quotes an article in the *Harvard Business Review* from February about how "employees in managerial and professional roles, are taking their own unpaid sabbaticals when their organizations fail to offer them." They studied professionals who took sabbaticals and found that "people largely experienced significant, positive changes in their work and life." I suppose starting Rep Methods was, in fact, a sabbatical—a change of pace, a move in a different direction from where I came. According to Tish, "In general, sabbaticals are extended periods of time, spanning anywhere from two months to a year, during which one can change her duties and pace of work. Rest is often a key part of sabbaticals, but they are not long vacations, so nix any fantasy about sipping piña coladas on a beach for months."[5] No piña coladas over here! This is a working sabbatical and one in which I will return to the selling world with a refreshed approach.

In 2017, Ryan Stewman wrote an article on LinkedIn about salespeople's mental health. Although the article is slightly androcentric, it has some interesting perspectives on mental health, addiction, and salespeople. Ryan is a badass sales coach and a like-minded human. Interestingly, Ryan cites

---

5   Tish Harrison Warren, "Can Everyone Take a Sabbatical? We All Need a Rest," *The New York Times,* June 25, 2023, https://www.nytimes.com/2023/06/25/opinion/sabbatical-work-life-balance.html.

studies to show salespeople are at serious risk for addiction and addictive behaviors.

It makes sense. We often live and breathe for the "sales kill"; we "race" for the chase. Many of us are endorphin addicts! Depending on what you sell—houses, mortgages, cars, stones, clothes, or software—you can experience many negativities while you push to find those yeses and fight the nos. Ryan makes a successful point in his article. "We like to pretend everything's okay, but our subconscious can only take so much abuse before the mind fights back. Sometimes the mind can fight back with rage, anxiety, and other emotions that can cost us sales. So naturally, we look to suppress the ability of our subconscious to start that fight. Often, the fundamental suppression mechanisms are alcohol, marijuana, drugs, cigarettes, caffeine, and pills.[6]" The bottom line: sales reps need to be careful, and we need to pay attention to these coping mechanisms. We must find an outlet for our stress relief.

As you read through the previous chapters, I hope you realized how salespeople rely on emotional connections, relationships, emotional intelligence, and empathy, and above all, we need balance. Are we more emotionally invested in our customers than in friends or family? Are we addicted to winning? Are we using improper coping mechanisms? Salespeople must recognize and address unhealthy behavior

---

6   Ryan Stewman, "Why Substance Abuse and Salesmen Often Go Hand in Hand," LinkedIn, October 27, 2017, https://www.linkedin.com/pulse/why-substance-abuse-salesmen-often-go-hand-ryan-stewman/.

to change it and have a sustainable career. Too often we get burned out, myself included. I hope to inspire new attitudes toward mental health and sales practices.

If you or someone else you know needs help, please reach out. You are not alone. There is hope, and there is help. No one needs to suffer alone or be afraid to change. There are programs designed to help people like us work through these improper coping mechanisms and begin to heal. Recovery is possible.

Good luck out there, and maybe I'll get to train with you someday. Better yet, I'll see you on the show floor selling! Look for me at a surfaces industry trade show and say hello! Stay healthy, friends, and keep selling! #repmethods #stonegirlsrock

Acknowlededements

Mentors

Sarah Blakley
Annette Dean Olsen
Prudence Santore
Freddie Meyer
Patty Dominguez
Phil Devore
Brad Hanner
Alberto Antolini
Tiziana Bellantuoni
Sonny Esses
Jaslene Sawhney
Mike Brown
Katie Jensen

Thank you

Rep Methods

We Make Order Makers, Not Order Takers

Alison
Mullins

Cultivated Creator & Stone Lover

My roots are in Appalachia,
although you might find me
wandering in a quarry
somewhere around the
world. My passion for selling
comes from these
mountains.

Keep on Rocking!
#stonegirlsrock

✿ Rep Methods

We Make Order Makers, Not Order Takers

Work with us in 3 steps.

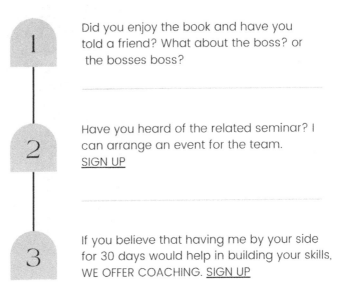

1 Did you enjoy the book and have you told a friend? What about the boss? or the bosses boss?

2 Have you heard of the related seminar? I can arrange an event for the team. SIGN UP

3 If you believe that having me by your side for 30 days would help in building your skills, WE OFFER COACHING. SIGN UP

⚙ Rep Methods

We Make Order Makers, Not Order Takers

You Made it! Great job on finishing the book!
I appreciate your time and hope you found it valuable.
If you think someone you know could benefit from this
book, please consider passing it along. I would love to
be referred to them.
Finally, if you have a few moments, leaving us a review
online would be greatly appreciated. At Rep Methods,
our goal is to provide the best possible help and
support to our clients.

Alison

⚙ Rep Methods

We Make Order Makers, Not Order Takers

selfpublishing.com

NOW IT'S YOUR TURN

Discover the EXACT 3-step blueprint you need to become a bestselling author in as little as 3 months.

Self-Publishing School helped me, and now I want them to help you with this FREE resource to begin outlining your book!

Even if you're busy, bad at writing, or don't know where to start, you CAN write a bestseller and build your best life. With tools and experience across a variety of niches and professions, Self-Publishing School is the <u>only</u> resource you need to take your book to the finish line!

DON'T WAIT

Say "YES" to becoming a bestseller:
https://selfpublishing.com/friend/

Follow the steps on the page to get a FREE resource to get started on your book and unlock a discount to get started with SelfPublishing.com

We Make Order Makers, Not Order Takers